Planning and Building a Conservatory

THE COMPLETE HANDBOOK

PAUL HYMERS

NEW HOLLAND

DEDICATION

For my sister Anne:
hope you get your conservatory one day!

First published in 2005 by New Holland Publishers (UK) Ltd
Garfield House, 86–88 Edgware Road
London W2 2EA
United Kingdom
London • Cape Town • Sydney • Auckland
www.newhollandpublishers.com

1 3 5 7 9 10 8 6 4 2

ISBN 1 84330 910 6

Senior Editor: Corinne Masciocchi
Editor: Ian Keary
Designer: Casebourne Rose Design Associates
Illustrator: Sue Rose
Cover photograph and jacket design: AG&G Books

Reproduction by Modern Age Repro, Hong Kong
Printing by Kyodo Printing Co, Singapore

ACKNOWLEDGEMENTS

With thanks to everyone who has allowed me to visit their conservatories,
to my colleagues past and present, and to Kevin and Steve in the Print Unit,
for their manuscript-copying services on this and previous books.
Many thanks to Hartwell Architects for providing the plans on pages 58 and 59.

DECLARATION

The views expressed in this book are those of the author and
do not necessarily reflect those of his employers.

The cover photograph features a conservatory by S&A Double Glazing Ltd,
111 Hopewell Drive, Chatham, Kent ME5 7NP Tel: 01634 843148

Contents

Introduction

IT'S MARCH and the sun is new and bright, but outside the wind is bitingly cold and flattening the daffodils, so you can't stay out and enjoy it. Unless that is, you have a conservatory. In a conservatory, summer comes early and you get to escape the dry, fake heat of central heating long before everyone else and bask in the hidden warmth of the sun.

The hardest thing of all can be deciding to what use you would most like to put your glazed addition. Conservatories are different things to different people – for many, they are greenhouses attached to the home, and in them a miniature jungle of exotic plants and flowers can be nurtured; for others, the space is a playroom for the children or a dining room in which to entertain. Some will take the recreational space to the extreme and use it to house a plunge or spa pool – and when you think about it, what a perfect environment conservatories make for all the pleasures of relaxation. You might even decide that you need to divide your conservatory into different zones with an internal glazed partition or, better still, build more than one.

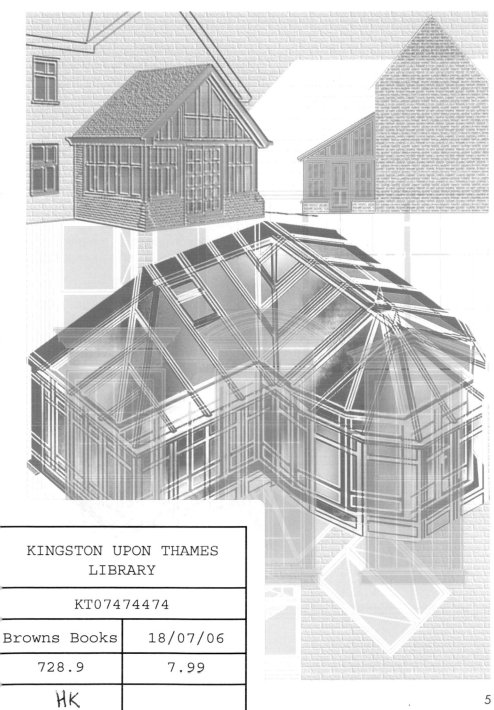

CHAPTER ONE

Preliminaries

According to one report, within the first 18 months of a new home's life, one in five houses has been extended by a conservatory. Whether this statistic is accurate or not, one thing is true: it seems that almost everybody wants a home with a conservatory at some point in their life. Conservatories suit our temperate climate perfectly, and bring us as near to the garden as we can be when the weather stops us being actually in it.

At least 265,000 people thought so in 2002 when they installed conservatories in their homes. That figure, compared with the 1998 total of 180,000, shows a 45 per cent growth and explains why almost one third of all windows and doors made in that year were destined for a conservatory. The growth continued in 2003, and so long as home improvement grows, conservatory additions seem likely to grow with it.

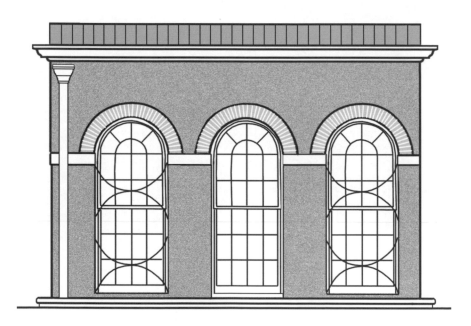

A detached orangery with arch-headed sash windows

Breweries and restaurateurs know this all too well, and if a pub has a garden these days, the chances are that it will have a conservatory too. Conservatories are at the centre of our care homes in later life, and on the grandest scale imaginable they are at the top of our tourist attractions in the Eden Project, where the geodesic bubble structures, the individual biospheres that hold rainforests, are as tall as 11 double-decker buses. Even in the city centre of Sheffield, among prime retail space a 21 m-high conservatory built in 2002 stands as a public winter garden free for everyone's enjoyment.

Your budget might not stretch to the Eden Project's £80,000,000 or the Sheffield Winter Garden's £5,500,000, but a conservatory on a home is still a microclimate and the pleasure of using it will be just as great.

The evolution of the conservatory

Conservatories aren't modern inventions; they've been with us

An orangery extension with 18th-century Georgian sash windows

7

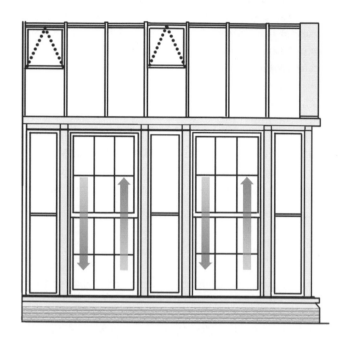

Traditional 19th-century style conservatory with
sash windows for low and high level ventilation

since the 18th century and were
extremely popular with our forebears,
so adding a conservatory to a period
or even a listed or historic home isn't
inappropriate at all. The design and
materials, however, should be
appropriate to your home and its
architecture and time.

The modern conservatory is often
built and used as a cheaper form of
extension, to provide extra space in
our smaller homes of today, but the
true origins and definition of the
conservatory relate to plants and their
propagation, the evolution of which
began with the orangery.

From the late 16th century, when
exotic plants were first introduced to
Britain from warmer climes, the
problem of wintering them had to be

addressed, and the first orangeries were built to house orange trees. Mostly they were built detached from grander homes in the Renaissance style; with solid wood frames and symmetrical windows evenly spaced apart although with solid roofs, covered in lead or slates, they let in little light for growth. In winter they were often heated by stoves to keep the plants alive until the risk of frost passed and they could be moved outside again. Developments in growing exotics meant that when orangeries were heated through winter, all kinds of fruits and plants could be grown, from orchids and pineapples to peaches and grapes.

A lot of people thought orangeries best placed in the garden, against a wall rather than attached to the house, although you occasionally see one linked to an historic house by a lobby, as a kind of architectural compromise. The orangery, a building of some substance, was really set to evolve into the greenhouse of less substance.

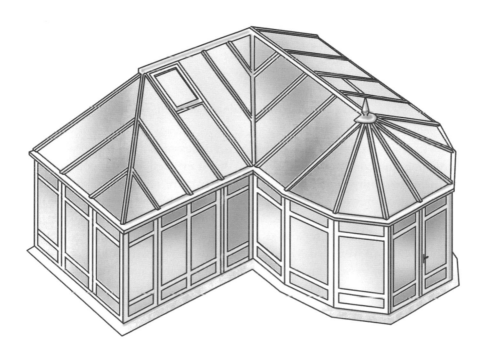

21st-century PVC-u 'Victorian style' conservatory

Orangery windows framed with stone surrounds

The Victorians were extremely fond of gardening, and conservatories gave them the opportunity to do it all year around and grow newly discovered exotics. The buildings could be attached, linked or entirely separated from the home, but were usually close to it and were not to be confused with the greenhouse, which like the potting shed, was a workhouse. The conservatory got its name at this point in time, although orangeries were still being built in the traditional brick-walled and solid-roofed way. The orangery may have been the predecessor, but it isn't correct to say that it evolved into the conservatory – the two are, and always have been, separated by architecture, if not use.

The first conservatories were simple lean-to timber-framed designs, but once wrought iron took over from cast iron, metal frames appeared and with them bigger and grander designs. The sections could even be curved, and some more graceful architecture was popular, a mile removed from the standard lean-to box. The Palm House at Kew Gardens, built in 1848, is a prime example of

Replica Tuscan-style window surrounds, cast in resin stone, can be used
in orangery or garden room architecture to achieve a classical look

Full height
window with
lower panel

Dwarf wall

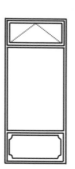

Fielded panel

Full height window

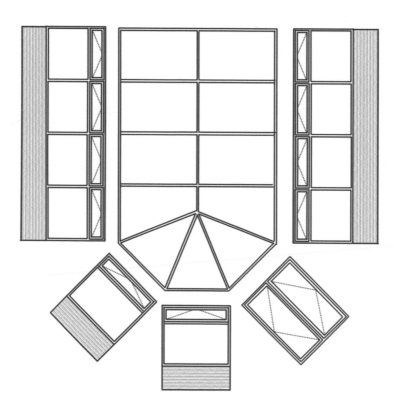

Exploded view of the elements for conservatory design

what you can do with a little bit of curved iron, although you might not want to work to this scale on your own.

The Victorian middle classes started to add on conservatories in the latter half of the 19th century, after the Window Tax had gone and glass became more available in larger and cheaper panes. They used conservatories just as the upper classes did, for growing tender and exotic plants, albeit smaller ones, preferring to separate them from the living areas of the home – not for reasons of energy conservation (of which they were blissfully unaware), but in order to keep out the musty smell of damp earth and humidity. Even crammed full of plants, conservatories were perfect places to entertain, and owners made sure that they were well ventilated and fitted with shades to control the temperature.

The Edwardians enjoyed conservatory life too, but for them World War One ended the pleasure, and after that the Great Slump made them too expensive to build and maintain to be worthwhile. Not until the late 1970s did the conservatory find its way back into our lives, and then it was ready to be something completely different. Double-glazing was on the horizon.

With the advent of sealed double-glazing and aluminium windows in the late 1970s, conservatories grew in popularity. From timber-stained double-glazed windows in the early 1980s to PVC-u, they continued to grow and reach a peak in the mid-1990s. The peak doesn't seem to be dropping yet, and conservatories remain as popular as ever today, partly due to the fact that they were exempted from the Building Regulations in 1985, because they couldn't keep up with the ever-increasing standards for thermal insulation. Most conservatories since then have been built without planning or Building Regulation controls, and are constructed to a lower standard than the home to which they are attached.

Conservatory supply-and-build companies

The replacement window industry was, and to some extent still is, haunted by cowboy companies who change their names as frequently as they change people's windows. The industry was totally unregulated until 2002, when the work was introduced in some aspects to the Building Regulations. Companies can self-certify their work if they belong to FENSA, but this doesn't extend to conservatories, which remain largely exempt from control of any kind in England and Wales.

Some of the cowboys, I fear, have moved in from replacement windows. You can find some protection against them with a few simple measures.

13

Recommendation

Check with neighbours, friends, colleagues and relatives who have had a conservatory built, to see if they can recommend a firm.

The Conservatory Association and the Glass and Glazing Federation (GGF) are trade bodies that seek to regulate their members and achieve higher standards in the industry. To some extent they have been successful, particularly the GGF, which has virtually created a self-regulating industry from its members in respect of the supply and fitting of glass. Their rules mirror the Building Regulation requirements and British Standard advice, and they have tended to precede the introduction of the former, at least in respect of safety glass and insulation.

Certification, FENSA and Building Control

The FENSA (Fenestration Self-Assessment Scheme) system was created in April 2002, when Building Regulations were amended to include this work – rather late in the day, since it had been enjoying unregulated growth (over 2,000,000 installations a year) for the previous 20 years, but you can't rush into these things, can you? The industry had been more or less unregulated before then.

To avoid the prospect of having every replaced window in the country inspected by council Building Control Officers, the industry brought in the FENSA scheme as a self-

certification system by which it could regulate itself and avoid having to make applications for Building Regulation Approval. FENSA does not, therefore, have much relevance to conservatories – except perhaps as an indication of a company's financial health and ability to self-regulate itself in window replacement – something which it can't do for the construction of a conservatory.

FENSA inspectors do carry out the odd spot check on their members' work to see if they are complying with the regulations. They would normally add a fee on to their estimate to cover the cost of FENSA registration, but since this doesn't relate to conservatories you shouldn't have to pay it. Check to make sure it hasn't been slipped in by mistake.

Some installers are also able to offer you insurance before they start the job. This takes the form of a money-back warranty if they cease to trade or if there are defects with the materials or workmanship. Since the warranty should be independent, it is worth taking it out if you can afford to.

Pay by credit card

The Credit Protection Act gives you some protection, making a credit card the safest method of payment. If you have paid a deposit to a contractor who then goes out of business before starting the work, the Act should allow you to recover the payment.

If the contractor doesn't have a credit card scheme, you might ask for a deposit indemnity. If it is a limited company, its directors should be able to provide it, and if it isn't limited, the proprietor should. Of course, you must remember that the indemnities will only work if you can locate these people personally – and that may not be a good use of your time, or easy if the firm has gone bust.

If you are paying by credit, whether by card or by loan, including situations in which the contractor is acting as the broker, as some package firms do, you have rights under the Consumer Credit Act 1974. These rights extend to changing your mind shortly after signing, if:

● The credit loan is between £50 and £15,000 and isn't secured by your plot/home.

● You signed the credit agreement after discussing the details face to face with the contractor.

● You signed at home or anywhere other than the contractor's offices or premises.

You should have been given a copy of the agreement, which sets out your rights to cancel it, and you should receive a second copy in the post at a later stage. Be warned, however, that the time limits in which to do so are quite tight.

Other benefits of contractor credit finance include extra protection measures against the contractor where he is in breach of contract or misrepresentation. This still applies even if the contractor is acting as the broker, and means that the lender is equally liable for any claim you have against the contractor in these respects. Even if the contractor goes bust before he starts the job, taking your deposit with him, you will have redress here. The contract sum needs to fall between £100 and £30,000, so this could exclude general contractors but should apply to individual trade contractor arrangements.

Installer warranties

Installers who belong to trade federations such as the GGF or FENSA advertise the fact as a symbol of their professionalism or quality of work. You should be aware that all such groups exist to represent the interest of their members, the tradesmen, as well as their customers. Not all companies advertise honestly; indeed, a report released in 1996 suggested that 13–22 per cent of all building firms made false declarations about membership of trade associations.

When you do find a bona fide member, check to see if they can also offer a warranty for their work that guarantees you – normally for a period of up to 10 years from the date of completion – against financial loss arising from any defects with inferior workmanship or materials, and against the event of the contractor becoming insolvent, or dying, before finishing the work. With these policies, you can expect that if you seriously fall out with your contractor in the middle of the job, a refereeing service should be provided to arbitrate between you, and if necessary an alternative contractor can be appointed to finish the job. This situation would also apply if the contractor went bankrupt, died or simply disappeared before finishing the work.

Warranties are insurance policies like any other. You pay a fee that is often somewhere between 1 and 2 per cent of the contract sum, and you are covered against particular misadventures for 10 years or so. You can also expect to be protected against the loss of a deposit paid to the installer. Make sure that the cover extends to sub-contractors or nominated suppliers engaged in the project by your contractor, such as electricians or plumbers; not many installers complete work these days without using some sub-contracted labour somewhere along the way.

Although the cost of all this insurance will not be insignificant, it is the price you pay for peace of mind in an industry that is unregulated and fraught with problems of disputes and poor workmanship. In time, perhaps the 'free insurance' currently enjoyed with some materials will be extended to all qualified tradesmen.

CHAPTER TWO

Design and materials

PVC-u in all the styles

Since the 1980s the standard material for conservatories has been plastic: a frame of unplasticized polyvinyl chloride double-glazed windows and polycarbonate roof sheets.

PVC-u windows have looked better in white ever since the material became resistant to ultraviolet light and its fading ability, and this is still by far the popular choice. For those of us who prefer the appearance of wood

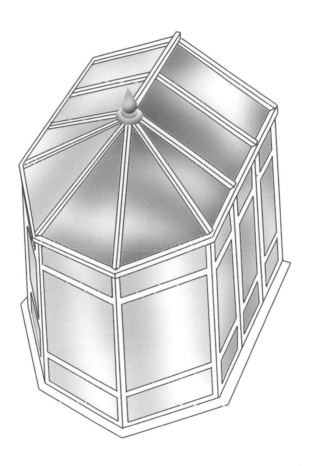

A popular three-sided hip-end PVC-u model

A square hip-ended PVC-u model with finial on ridge

without the maintenance bit, PVC-u can be bought with a GRP skin embedded with a timber-lookalike grain. You can have a choice of oak, mahogany or whatever else in a warp-, rot-, bow-, split-, swell- or shrink-free material. No, it doesn't look like the real thing, but it doesn't need painting, either. (I'm inclined to think this timber-effect plastic is well suited to front doors, but somehow it's too much for windows and much too much for fascias.)

From an environmental view, this material may well turn into the 21st century's ultimate nightmare. When timber gets old it kindly rots away, quietly and without fuss – even before then, you can saw it up into shavings and recycle it as one of many

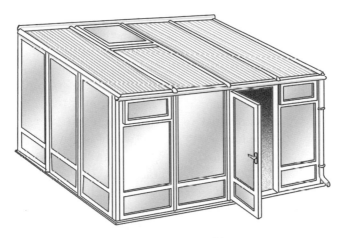

A lean-to PVC-u model

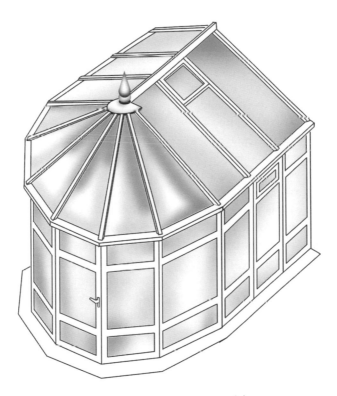

A hexagonal end PVC-u model

by-products, with very little energy being expended. If you bury it in a landfill site, it eventually returns to the soil like a fallen tree.

Plastic is different – chemically produced for durability, it will never rot or degrade. Some plastics that have been subjected to accelerated ageing in laboratories have indicated that if you bury them in the ground you could come back 10,000 years later and dig them up. When you think about how many PVC-u frames there are in our homes now, you begin to see how this could be a problem for the future. The homes in which they reside may last 100 years or more, and during that time the glass will have to be changed several times, and the fixings and hinges will have rusted and broken too. It's more likely that our desire to continually improve our homes will see the windows of today being replaced in 20 years with newer models.

And what are we going to do with all that plastic? It can't be burned without giving off nasty gases and accelerating the greenhouse effect with carbon dioxide release, and it certainly can't be buried in landfill sites, which traditionally is what we've been doing with all our unwanted material. It can only be recycled, and as yet, we haven't that much of a need for old PVC. Already we have seen how new legislation makes old windows redundant – and by old I mean those made prior to

2002. Before this date, the U value of standard double-glazing was less and the glass was hence thinner, so windows can't be relocated in a new opening and can't always be reglazed to take thicker glass; the chances of re-employing a 1980s window somewhere else are very unlikely.

Twenty years on, the technology has improved not so much in the materials as the system of putting them together. With the base and dwarf wall constructed, the rest of the PVC-u structure can comfortably be erected within a week. (*See* System build *on page 115.*)

The marketing of PVC-u in replacement windows and conservatories remains, well – enthusiastic. Given the basis that the product is maintenance-free and there for life, we have fallen in love with PVC-u. 'Maintenance-free' is, however, stretching the truth a bit too far. For one thing, the glass used in double-glazing has a shelf life which can be surprisingly short at the cheaper end of the market. Double-glazing has a cavity that is now typically 20 mm wide between the panes and is hermetically sealed around the edges. The seals tend to break down and moisture gets in to the cavity, resulting in the windows misting up between the panes. Only one solution exists when this happens – replace them. Most of the cost in PVC-u now derives from the glass, and reglazing a window may not be significantly cheaper than replacing one. This is a fault with the glass, and it can happen to double-glazing in timber windows in just the same way.

Another common fault comes from the sliding mechanism in the friction scissor hinges. The plastic pins, which can be tightened for friction resistance, slide along a steel channel until they perish and snap in two, bringing the casement out of square with the frame.

These maintenance issues are redeemable, but compare how many companies you know in the window maintenance business with how many you know in the conservatory and window replacement business. Plastic windows have become disposable, and clearly that needs to change. If, after 30 years or so, they do have to be replaced, let us hope that the product can be recycled without too much energy being burned, as the prospect of a plastic window mountain building up is not a pleasant one.

You can choose from several packaged PVC-u designs or create your own. If you go for the latter option, remember that windows and doors come in standard sizes at greatly reduced prices, and also that polycarbonate roof sheets are modular. Designing your addition using these modular dimensions will save a great deal on waste and cost.

Most roof sheets are 500 mm wide, allowing for bars (because they fit to glazing bars, the width of these is taken into account) plus a starter bar width. If the starter bar is 50 mm, two sheets will get you a conservatory width of 1050 mm, six sheets 3050 mm and 10 sheets 5050 mm. In many ways it pays to find your products before you finalise your design.

Aluminium frames

Aluminium window and door frames are less common in the home improvement market, where plastic dominates. In the 1970s and early 1980s it was recognised as a strong, durable and quality product, but somehow lost its way – something to do with the fact that the window frames were often in fact sub-frames surrounded by hardwood and looked a little incongruous, even then. Later, when powder-coated aluminium that looked like PVC-u came in, it felt cold to the touch and suffered from surface condensation.

Aluminium framing has been developed a bit since those days, and most commercial buildings – shops, restaurants, offices, etc – which have high insulation standards to meet are fitted with them.

Aluminium only ever comes in two finishes – anodised and polyester powder-coated. Anodising is an electro-chemical process that creates a tough oxide finish, physically altering the surface of the metal and accidentally giving it a high resistance to electric current. Anodised aluminium door handles that you see in commercial buildings may be your only experience of this finish in its SAA (satin anodised aluminium) finish form. Dyes can be added to the process when the metal is porous, so colourful frames can be created that look nothing like cheap ironmongery.

Polyester powder coatings spray-applied in the factory offer a perfect smooth finish that is consistent in both colour and texture. It also offers excellent resistance to ultraviolet light (something which plastic doesn't generally excel at), and if it gets scratched it can be repaired in situ (again, something that plastic can't excel at).

Timber frames and windows

Not so very long ago all windows were wood – hard to believe, isn't it? Even in my apprenticeship with a local builder in the early 1980s we used standard-sized softwood timber windows and doors on all our new developments. Painting had grown out of fashion then, and timber parts weren't primed in the factory ready to be undercoated and glossed, as they had been before. Instead, they came off the lorry base decorated with a light stain and were top-coated with stain on site. Painting in the site store shed, trying to avoid running or collecting paintbrush hairs, was all part of the fun. The joinery companies (they still exist) had catalogues full of standard off-the-shelf models in different styles. But plastic was just around the corner.

Timber windows still exist, but their market share has been reduced a fair bit since then – all of which may change because timber has its own advantages – and guess what? It can even be coated with a white polyurethane finish to make it look like the other PVC-u windows in your home. Here, you get the solid strength, insulation and environmental soundness of wood without that maintenance problem we call painting.

Whichever timber you use, you can make sure it comes from a managed and sustainable source by looking for the FSC (Forest Stewardship Council) label. This isn't the world's only system of reducing deforestation, but it is the most high-profile.

At the bottom end of the timber market comes softwood pine, usually from Scandinavia or Canada, where it grows slowly in cold climates to produce timber of close grain and high strength. All pine used in construction comes from these areas, even the stuff used for garden sheds.

Where timber takes over from other materials is in the detail. Because it is a very easily worked material, fine sections can be carved that remain comparatively strong. Glazing beads can be cut in windows that exactly match the originals, and in period homes these originals can be quite slender. It doesn't necessarily

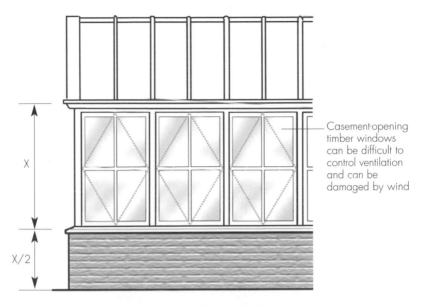

Casement-opening timber windows can be difficult to control ventilation and can be damaged by wind

Lower walls can achieve the right balance of proportion with the windows

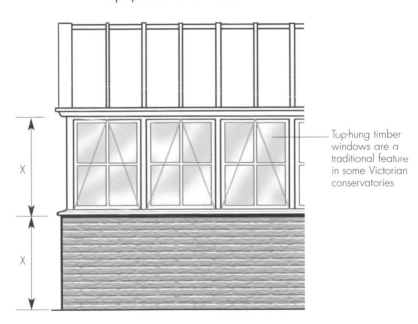

Top-hung timber windows are a traditional feature in some Victorian conservatories

Higher walls can dramatically change the balance of proportion making the windows too short and fat

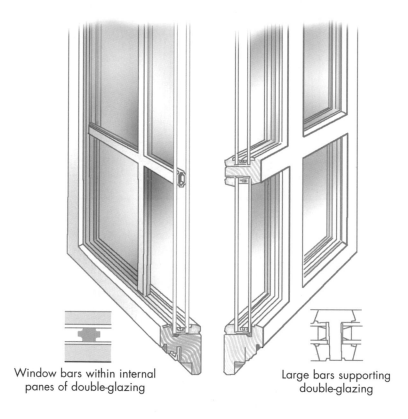

Window bars within internal
panes of double-glazing

Large bars supporting
double-glazing

Double-glazing and timber bars

mean you're forced to have single-glazing either, because the bars can be superficially planted on today's 24 or 26 mm-thick sealed units. Seeing the window square on, you won't notice a difference, but if you can reduce the depth of the unit to 18 mm, it will help when you look at an angle. 20 mm clear glass sealed units were standard in the 1990s, made up of two 4 mm panes beside a 12 mm cavity; a decade earlier, the cavities were down to 8 and even 6 mm. The growth in the thickness of double-

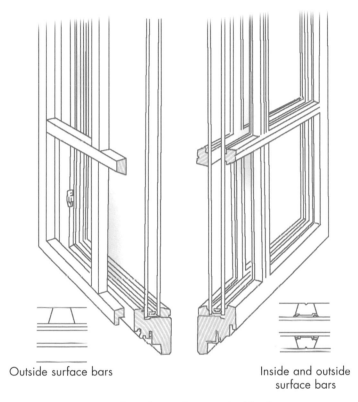

Outside surface bars

Inside and outside
surface bars

Dummy timber glazing bars on double-glazing

glazed windows' air gaps is down to the ever-increasing standards for thermal insulation over this period, and until the advent of low-emissivity coatings and argon gas fillings, making it thicker was all that could be done to improve it.

Finished with a Georgian-style gable end, a timber-framed conservatory painted white with a single-glazed roof is in a league of its own. In my view nothing beats this in appearance, and structures like this are easily designed 6 or 7 m wide and

25

11 or 12 m long. If you can run to the expense of including a full cartwheel framed light or a semi-circular 'sunburst' window in the gable, it becomes even more impressive – in this form, your glass extension becomes a classic piece of architecture, a mile away from the bolt-on plastic box model.

The range of hardwoods used for framing is necessarily restricted to ensure that only wood sourced from sustainable forests is used. Most hardwoods are tropical, from either West Africa or Indonesia, and particularly in the case of the latter, the rate at which tropical forests are disappearing is alarming, and is terminal for many species.

Idigbo is a West African species of high strength wood that has a high natural resistance to fungal attack and rot: you don't get to evolve in the humid tropical forests of the Ivory Coast without having some genetic preservation built in. In the table below, Young's Modulas of Elasticity allows us to see the relationship between stress and strain in any given section. The higher the E value, the stronger the timber.

With a timber of higher strength, you can use a smaller section of frame and mullions, to suit an Edwardian fenestration style, for example.

Oak frames and barn styles

Extending onto a converted barn or similarly styled home may lead you towards an oak-framed conservatory or sun room. Oak and glass go very well together, at least aesthetically. Using oversized chunky framing between the windows and a generous sole and head plate above and below them, a roof of any material can be supported. Green oak is surprisingly soft and workable, and regularised sections can be carved with stop chamfers and subtle details. With an oak frame you'll want to enjoy the conservatory from both the inside and outside, and this wood is best finished with some gentle beeswaxing to bring out the beautiful grain and colour.

There are really only two choices for any dwarf walls with an oak frame, the first being none at all, sitting the sole plate directly on to the damp-proof course (DPC) for a fully glazed wall design. This could well be the most suitable, but it's important to make sure that you have at least two courses of bricks beneath the DPC above ground level. This 150 mm will ensure that rain splashing doesn't soak the sole plate on a regular basis, thus shortening its life expectancy.

Young's Modulas comparison

Softwood	.7300
Brazilian mahogany	.8600
Idigbo	.9300

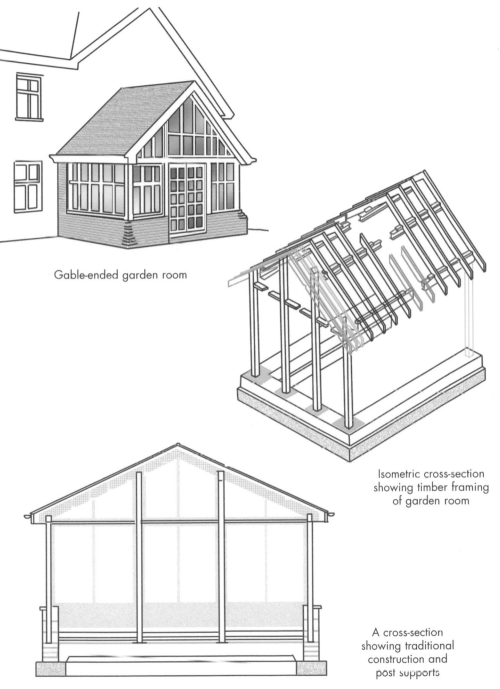

Gable-ended garden room

Isometric cross-section
showing timber framing
of garden room

A cross-section
showing traditional
construction and
post supports

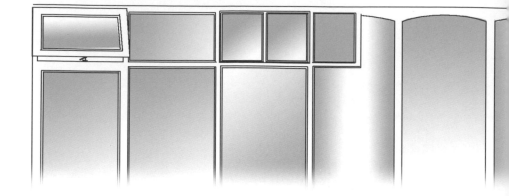

Window head styles

The second choice is to have a short dwarf wall of perhaps just three or four courses of bricks above the DPC; however, it doesn't work well to have high brick walls with a squat oak frame sitting on them – the proportions and beauty of oak dictate that it should be by far the most prominent material after the glass.

Extending any converted barn presents a design challenge in trying to maintain the agricultural look, but it is possible. The main rules are to try to maintain the scale and grandeur of the existing structure in the individual elements of your addition, regardless of its size – in other words, if you have planning permission only for a small addition, don't scale down the detailing in empathy, but keep it in sync with the original.

Look to using handmade secondhand roof tiles and bricks that blend in with the existing ones, and resist the urge to create too much hard landscaping outside if it isn't there already. Most barn additions blend in better with green landscaping, rather than with decks or patios.

If your barn home has a curvaceous, plain tiled roof, trying to tie in a die-straight glass one to it is always going to be a problem. It is far better to intersect the two roofs with the same material, and if you still want a glazed roof on your new room, switch to glass at the plane of the wall line or beyond. Cross tie beams that restrain your wall plates can be an architectural feature, whether you need them or not in this timber, and you may even want to install knee braces at the post and tie beam junctions to replicate barn aisle details.

There are specialist companies who design and build in oak, using

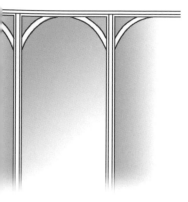

Conservatories on period homes

Walk around any housing development or down any street in Britain, and you'll see that almost all conservatories erected today are made of PVC-u in the style described by their manufacturers as 'Victorian'. They are popular, although there isn't much that is truly Victorian (in architecture or materials) about them. With a framed hexagonal end they tend to comprise one pair of French doors, fixed windows with a fanlight on every single window, and a very low-pitched roof decorated with an ornate ridge and finial. Regardless of how they are named, the style has hit the nail on the head as far as consumer demand goes, as they add a bit of style and finesse to the design of many homes, particular those built in the last half of the 20th century, as

traditional methods of jointing without metal fixings. Admittedly, they tend to specialise in new homes or detached outbuildings (barn-style garages, for instance), but they will have the expertise you'll be looking for that other builders and carpenters won't.

Gable-end conservatory addition with a lower roof pitch

Without upper floor windows above the conservatory, the roof pitch
can be increased to add height. The depth should be restricted
to avoid the glazed sides from appearing too dominant.

well as providing the owners with space and light, probably the two most important wishes of homeowners today.

On Listed Buildings or in Conservation Areas, it just might be possible to find a PVC-u-framed and double-glazed design that is acceptable to both you and the Planning Department, but the chances are that it won't. Traditional materials and construction methods have become a bit lost for many buildings, but conservatories can to a large extent be built to replicate them.

Glass

Victorian conservatories of the 19th century either had a timber or cast-iron frame with a brick or stone plinth beneath the windows. The window glass came in relatively small panes and was single-glazed. The float glass panes often regarded as traditional did not become widely manufactured until the 1960s, revolutionising glass manufacture. 'Float' is a literal description of the manufacturing process, where a molten glass ribbon comes out of the kiln and floats over a bath of liquid tin, the result being a highly polished and smooth plate of glass that can be cut on the production line without any further preparation.

Before then and from the 1920s to this time, glass was rolled and drawn in a continuous process. During the 19th century, it was cast in sheets and known as plate glass, which is was what the Victorians and Edwardians used in their glazed additions, to begin with in smallish panes, but once the tax on glass was removed in 1845 and the demand for larger panes grew, sheets of 1050 x 250 mm were soon manufactured in this form, and these dimensions would replicate appropriately on a property of this era.

Even if you settle for single-glazing, the appearance and manufacture of modern glass is quite different to how it was for the Victorians, and only specialist companies that produce handmade glass can help you if you truly want to match history's products on your period home. Even then, you may not be able to use it everywhere. The position of the glass will probably determine what is replica and what is contemporary. In critical locations, where it can meet with accidents, glazing must be of a safety type, such as toughened or laminated; critical locations are explored on page 39.

Windows and frames

The style of window that predominated in the Victorian era is the box sash, which was used in conservatories as well, probably interspersed by fixed frames. The need for good ventilation has always been recognised by gardeners, and double-hung sashes have the great advantage of being openable at both the top and the bottom without being blown shut in the wind. If they do have a drawback, it is that at first they were quite chunky in appearance, although in the Edwardian era they were to become much more slender. The fenestration detail and pane size can vary as well and should reflect that used on the house, whether it is six panes over six, four over four or two over two.

The 19th century also saw patents for casements and top-hung window openings. The latter were particularly used in conservatories and greenhouses as vents because they sheltered the opening from rain and drew in the fresh air from the bottom to circulate up and out through the roof vents. The side-hung casements that are standard today were much less popular for conservatory use then, as they were prone to the elements, especially the wind, and all too easily damaged. Today, friction hinges resist wind pressure.

Top-hung vents were always used for roofs, and were kept to a smaller size to limit their weight. Winding gear was normally installed to open and close them manually. Whether you choose low or high technology to operate yours, the vent size should still be limited to control the weight of the vent window. By 'low technology' I mean a long wooden pole with a hook on the end and a friction hinge on the frame to hold

it open. 'High technology' means electric window openings, which can be bought as stand-alone devices to fit most windows and wired to a switch, or even greenhouse opening vent devices that open up automatically when the temperature rises. Either will have a maximum weight of vent under which they will operate, and you should bear this in mind at the design stage when planning the vent sizes.

Double-glazing has the great advantage of adding both sound and thermal insulation, but it's often difficult to use this in traditional timber sash windows, or indeed any window that contains glazing bars. In the original design of these windows, the bars were thin and the glass was fixed by putty, but when housing a much thicker double-glazed pane, the bars must also be much thicker and timber beading must be used to hold them in. Dummy glazing bars formed in PVC-u between the panes or superficially glued onto the glass afterwards don't come anywhere close to being authentic. A competent glazier will be able to advise you of the minimum bar sizes and their style to suit any thickness of glass you propose.

Roofs

If you look at most conservatory roof designs, you might be forgiven for thinking that Victorian conservatories all had ornate ridges with elaborate finials at the apex of a low hexagonal-shaped end, with all the windows having a line of fanlight vents beneath the eaves, and with a transom beneath each one. In fact, conservatories of this era looked nothing like this design; instead, larger roof-to-wall windows interspersed with a few fanlights were more common, along with steeply pitched roofs with plain ridges.

Raising the roof pitch to 40° or even 50° will make the glass roof dominant on the elevation sides, but I don't see many instances where this looks out of place. If it does on your home and you still want to go for a steep roof, it may be enough to locate the conservatory away from the principal entrance and front elevation. A more discreet site for it may have to be found, ideally a rear or side gable end if the position of the first-floor windows will allow it. Even if the roof pitch differs, extending the home out from a gable wall with a scaled-down gable-ended addition always appears sympathetic.

Contemporary design

For most of us, contemporary design in conservatories invokes an image of a glass box, frameless and created by a system of total glazing, minus any solid walls or window frames. To achieve this, glass mullion systems are used to support the glass sheets. The glass box concept has advantages that make it increasingly appealing.

Your own design might use frameless glazing with clear silicone joints to weather the panes together or an independent structure (inside or out) on which pre-drilled holes allow the fixings to support the panes. The idea here is to have a wall-less structure that allows 100 per cent clear vision, the structural floor finish supporting the bottom edge of the glass panels.

Advantages of the contemporary glass box design

- You have an uninterrupted view.
- There is harmonious continuity in the materials used for structure and cladding.
- Glass is a stylish and durable low-maintenance material.
- You only need one supplier for materials.
- It comes as a design and supply, or design, supply and erect package.
- It's quick to build and requires no 'wet' trades above the base.

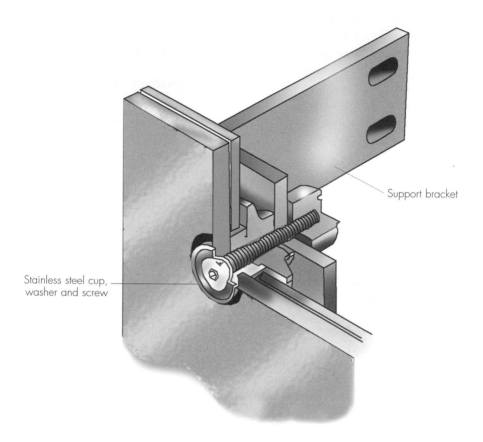

Support bracket

Stainless steel cup,
washer and screw

Frameless glazing with stainless
steel fixings to laminated glass

The base needs to be perfectly level, and to achieve a smooth and true surface, a power-floated finish to the concrete slab is best. If need be, you can cover it with a decorative surfacing of tiles or even floor paint directly, without having to add a layer of screed.

This design lends itself to the slab or raft-style foundation, which allows the concrete base to be shuttered with timber on the outside face and cast inside. For the slab to look presentable, the formwork shuttering should possess a good face that when removed (a process known as 'striking') reveals the face of the concrete as smooth and presentable. No dwarf brickwork wall or plinth needs to be used in this construction, although if the concrete hasn't come out looking as good as you might

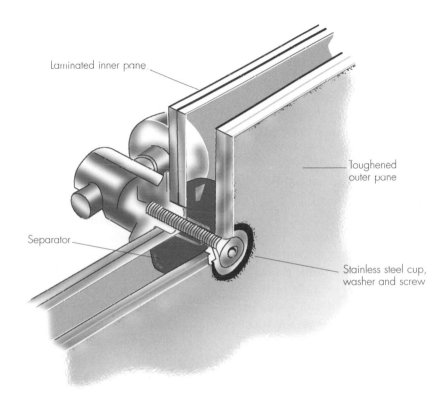

Laminated inner pane

Separator

Toughened
outer pane

Stainless steel cup,
washer and screw

Frameless glazing with double-glazing

have hoped, it can always be faced
with a brick skin around it, capped
off with a coping stone or course.

In some designs glass rafters and
glass piers can be used to support
the roof and wall panels, creating a
totally transparent structure with
no solid elements at all. This system
tends to work better in single-
glazing, which improves the
transparency of the appearance, but

it does mean that when not in
sunlight the room will only stay
few degrees above the outside air
temperature and could even drop
to freezing during a cold spell.

This kind of conservatory offers
the highest levels of vision
imaginable, and in many ways you
are in the garden. Where it becomes
noticeable that you are under glass is
when the sun shines through it: the

35

solar gain through single glazing is considerable, and the temperature can rise dramatically to 25°C and above in early spring sunshine, and 40°C in summer heat. A room on the extreme edge of the temperature range like this will have to be used differently: insulated doors to the existing home are essential to keep the cold out, but also to allow you to open them up and to let the sun's heat be distributed a little more fairly.

Contemporary design always works well with water gardens, where the combination of glass and reflective water can meet at the surface and blend together. A formal garden pond can be constructed right up to the edge of the glazed wall, giving you the chance to sit inside and watch the fish swim by – for the more adventurous water gardener, the pond can pass beneath the glazed wall and be half inside and half out so you can watch the fish swim under. The ultimate transition between home and garden, this design creates the opportunity for an ice-free pond zone and the chance to feed your pond fish from indoors. With the walls of the pond built to the right level the surface of the water can be kept at the bottom edge of the glass to avoid a cold draught at your feet. In warm weather, however, you can expect the water to evaporate and condense on the inside of the glass if it isn't well-ventilated, and this will mean both low- and high-level ventilation.

Curves and glass

The architectural effect of curved glass is impressive, and many aluminium framed lean-tos of the 1970s had curved panes at the eaves to make the transition from windows to rooflights. The reason we don't see them today is because of double-glazing: single glass sheets have, for at least a century, been capable of being made to curve if required relatively cheaply, but not so double-glazing.

Flat panes can also be glazed to a curved structure if the size and geometry of the curves are carefully calculated to achieve the appearance of curves in a faceted kind of way. You do need quite a large radius to pull this off successfully.

If you think you couldn't possibly live with a single-glazed conservatory, go and take a look at the Sheffield Winter Garden mentioned earlier. Constructed from 1,400 single panes, of which 140 are openable vents, the architecture of the building is a high inverted catenary arch, but the laminated glass panes are all deceptively flat, each with an aluminium frame carefully interlocking to the next one. This is a temperate conservatory with an underfloor heating system that is designed to merely keep the frost off in winter and that is fuelled from the city's sustainable grid. But it does show that a cool conservatory can have a function too.

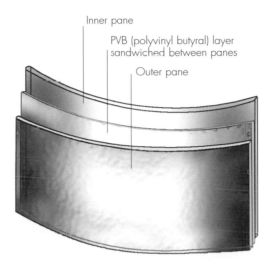

Inner pane

PVB (polyvinyl butyral) layer
sandwiched between panes

Outer pane

Curved laminated glass with a central layer
that absorbs impact and prevents it shattering

Glass

A single clear-glass pane 4 mm thick has the very best light transmittance, with 89 per cent of the UV light passing through it and 85 per cent of the solar heat falling in and transmitting through it. The problem is that heat transmittance is a two-way street, and a sheet of glass like this can't stop the heat leaving just as quickly as it arrived. A U value of 5.8 makes it one of the worst insulation products known to man.

If light transmittance through your roof is of no importance at all but you would rather have glass than a solid roof, you should go for green-tinted glass sheet. Green cuts down light more efficiently than any other shading colour, and a double-glazed unit with a 6 mm thick green glass outer pane will only let a mere 7 per cent of the light through. Silver reflective and bronze-shaded units, as used in designer-offices, are a very close second.

A standard double-glazed clear-glass unit of two 4 mm panes does quite well, with around 75 per cent of light penetrating, much better than polycarbonate sheeting; its solar heat transmission is also considerable, at 72 per cent.

If you're trying to keep out the heat of the sun, bronze-finished double-glazed units with thicker panes of 6 mm or 10 mm will repel all but 9 per cent of the sun's heat back at it.

Standard double-glazed unit with an hermetically-sealed air gap

Laminated glass bonded by plastic core layer

Toughened glass either in single-glazing or the inner pane of double-glazing for critical locations

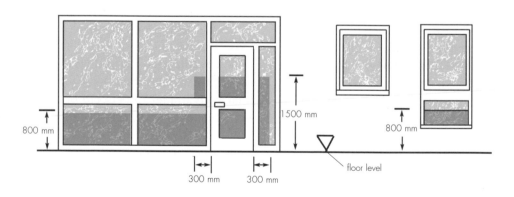

Toughened or laminated safety glass zones (shown darker)

The light transmission ability is about that percentage as well.

In terms of sound insulation, if you live beneath a flight path or beside a busy road, double-glazed units that employ a thick outer pane (the thicker the better) will achieve the best sound insulation – units with 12 mm thick outer panes are available. Sound is always best kept out with a combination of mass and an air cavity, and the heavier the product, the better: a double-glazed unit with a 12 mm outer pane, 12 mm cavity and 6 mm inner pane will weigh a staggering 45 kg/sq m, five times heavier than a single 4 mm float glass pane, and will require a great deal of structural support. For thermal insulation, argon-filled 20 mm cavities and low-e glass are about as good as you can get; and U values of down to 1.2 w/sq m deg k can be achieved.

Critical locations

For any conservatory to be exempted under the Building Regulations or approved, its glass in critical locations must be safety glass, which either resists breaking on impact or breaks safely. As far as most conservatories go, critical locations are pretty much everywhere. They are zones that are at risk from accidental collision by running children, sprawling adults, stumbling pensioners and so on. The diagram on page 38 should help to clarify this, but essentially they are found in any of the following zones:

1. Windows less than 800 mm above floor level.

2. Glass in doors up to 1500 mm above floor level*.

3. Glass in sidelights or windows within 300 mm beside a door and up to 1500 mm above floor level

* The issue regarding doors and sidelights of the maximum 1.5 m height only has effect in practice if largely solid doors are lit by vision panels above this level. In these cases, safety glass wouldn't be necessary.

Types of safety glass
Laminated glass
Laminated glass is one of those products that involve other materials combined with glass, namely transparent plastic. It is essentially two sheets of glass bonded on either side of a clear plastic sheet which holds it together on impact. Invented in 1909 by the French chemist Edouard Benedictus, it was given the product name of Triplex. Laminated glass will crack into fragments but remain in the frame, bonded together by its inner core; in this way it is harder to injure yourself by colliding with it and harder for intruders to break in by hitting it.

I get to see a fair number of dangerous structures caused by vehicles colliding unhappily with buildings, and I'm amazed at how well glass of this type hangs together after

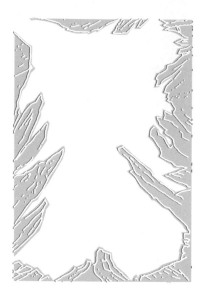

Float glass

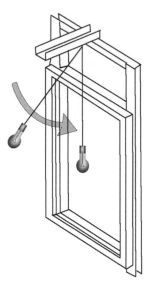

Laboratory impact test

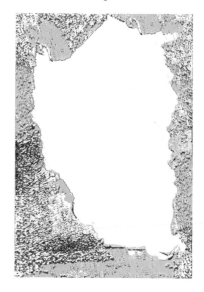

Toughened glass

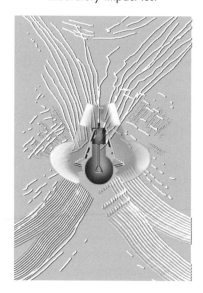

Laminated glass

Laboratory tests on glass reveal the risk from shards in ordinary panes.
Laminated and toughened glass breaks safely.

an impact. Recently called out by the police to a Mini-Metro v shop window dispute, I saw a car parked rakishly across the pavement with its rear half forming part of the window dressing and its front sticking out. I was impressed to note that rather than the glass shattering from the impact, as you might expect, the window frame and pane had been pushed into the shop but left standing. Despite being reversed into after a bad case of clutch slip, the floor-to-ceiling window had its frame broken and bowed, but the glass had only cracked around it. Even when the car was dragged out and the hole was boarded over, it stayed put.

The disadvantage of laminated glass is that it has no cavity for thermal insulation, and a single sheet of glass is already around 12 mm thick – great for car windscreens and shop windows, but not so great for double-glazing, where the insulating cavity is already pushing the pane width to the limits of acceptability.

Tempered glass

This product's arrival was born out of research carried out for the automobile industry in 1929. The laboratories of Saint-Gobain, France, were set the challenge of finding a stronger glass for car windows that would break safely. They discovered that by cooling glass rapidly from a temperature of 600° C down to 300° C, the glass become stronger, but when it did break it shattered into a very large number of tiny regular-sized fragments that were harder to cut yourself on. The rapid drop in temperature had to be achieved by blast-cooling in just a few short seconds, but it worked and the product became known as Securit glass. Tempered glass today is still widely found in buildings, mostly in the panes of glazed doors.

Toughened glass

By adding chemicals and controlling the process of manufacture, glass can become toughened to resist an impact. This is the material that most, if not all, of your windows should be fitted with. In a double-glazed pane often the inner sheet is the only toughened one, but since it can achieve this status in its production without requiring greater thickness or change in appearance, it has become the normal product in critical locations for double-glazing.

This does not mean to say that you won't have to specify it. The glazing industry tries hard to be self-regulating and mostly succeeds, but glass suppliers aren't clairvoyant and they may not guess that your windows are below 800 mm of the floor finish or beside a door if you don't tell them. When you are using a conservatory specialist or professional glazier, the onus of responsibility can reasonably be transferred to them, but with a DIY

Maximum pane size	Minimum thickness
WIDTH X HEIGHT	
250 x 2000 mm	6 mm
1100 x 1100 mm	8 mm
2250 x 2250 mm	10 mm
4500 x 3000 mm	12 mm
over 4500 x over 3000 mm	15 mm

build or a general builder the need arises to specify the glass type and to make sure that it complies before it's installed.

Safety glass comes with a British Standard kitemark or product label etched in the corner of a pane of glass that identifies the pane's nature. If there isn't one, it's not unreasonable to assume that it isn't anything but standard float glass. Apart from holding a receipt from a glass supplier who is a member of the Glass and Glazing Federation (GGF) and has some professional integrity, the only other way to check it is safely glass is with the use of a special eye-scope tool, as employed by glass suppliers, glaziers and surveyors. When held up to the surface of the glass, these little magnifying scopes can reveal what it is, and if a dispute arises over the issue, this is the only way of resolving it convincingly.

Annealed glass
Annealing glass is much the same process as tempering, in that the material is hardened by a sudden drop in temperature, but in this case its strength also comes from its thickness. Given enough thickness, annealed glass can be used for shop fronts, but in our homes it is reserved usually for the smallest of panes – a Georgian-style window or door where each pane is no larger than 0.5 sq m in area and 250 mm wide at the most. In these dimensions, annealed glass 6 mm thick will suffice, but in case you have plans to use it in larger panes, the table above will guide you to the minimum thickness you should use. Off the bottom of the scale are 4 mm-thick panes, which can only be used in traditional leaded or copper lights. Apart from this, 6 mm is the bare minimum that should be used.

Glass blocks

Not only are glass blocks inherently strong and suitable for use in critical locations, some have even been tested to periods of fire resistance and could be used for boundary walls.

Although they have been enjoying a period of revival since the Millennium, glass blocks have been around for some time, even though much of their past was spent in public conveniences, which makes it all the more remarkable that they should be so popular now. They are available in colours as well as clear, and their thickness creates an obscured light that is well suited to boundaries or privacy screens.

Glass blocks have a hollow core and come in a variety of thicknesses. You should use one of at least 200 mm, which has a weight of almost 100 kg/sq m for an external screen that is resistant to wind loads.

I always think that glass blocks look better when lit by artificial light from behind, from the outside looking in as it were. Daylight penetrates them in a considerably diffused way, but this in itself could be exactly what you are looking for on one elevation – what they don't do, of course, is offer you a view.

Sound insulation

Perhaps the worst performance of most conservatories comes not from insulation against heat but from sound. Polycarbonate roof sheets are to blame: they are excellent conductors of sound waves and can make a light shower of rain seem like a monsoon. Beneath a hailstorm, headphones would be in order, although you'd feel like you were wearing a crash helmet.

Double-glazing can offer good sound insulation but at a price. Within the domestic sector, sound insulation from double-glazing might be as high as 45 decibels (dB) in reduction of airborne sound. Specially supplied glass for those of us living near airports or busy roads could increase that to 55 dB. By comparison, an ordinary 4 mm-thick single-glazed window would typically reduce sound by 22 dB. If you aren't glazing the roof with double-glazing to similar standards, there is no point in doing the windows.

Sound is like water: it just finds the weak point in the structure and leaks in. To fully soundproof any room requires some attention to detail, such as sealing around joints and using quality windows that seal tightly; if just one PVC-u window has been pulled out of square by over-enthusiastic fitting, the sound insulation of your new room is lost by the tiniest of gaps between the frame and opening casement.

Along with sound insulation comes air permeability, or to you and I, draughts. Here, it is heat insulation that sets the controls, and European test standards set out just how much

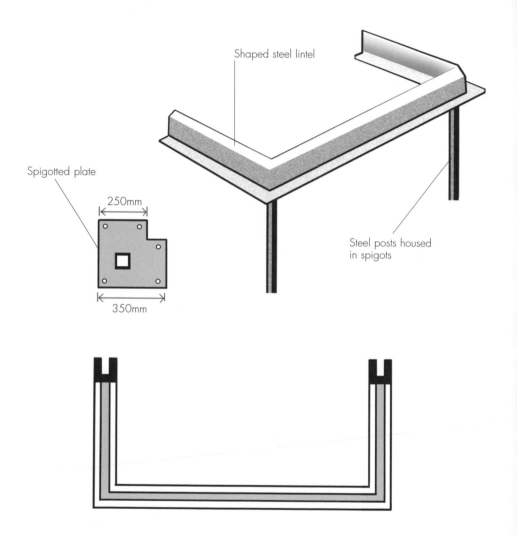

Shaped steel lintel

Spigotted plate

250mm

Steel posts housed
in spigots

350mm

Made-to-measure steel lintels are available for sun lounges

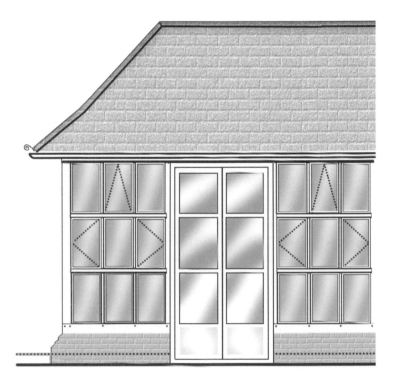

Garden rooms like this enjoy the benefit of
a solid roof shading but totally glazed walls

air should be allowed to pass through a closed window in one hour, given a gentle breeze outside.

Garden rooms and sun lounges

There is some mileage in looking to solid or at least partly solid roof coverings in lieu of glass on historic homes. Invariably the roof tiles are soft clay and textured like bricks, and the hard, straight lines of modern glass build into them uncomfortably. You can't make glazing look rustic or out of line, and so a transition between the two is needed. The intersecting roof of your new addition can be cut, pitched and tiled to match in with the old and at the same time create a visual buffer that will be more capable of accepting the glasswork. If the roof is more than 25 per cent unglazed, there may be a tendency to refer to it as a garden room or sun lounge rather than a conservatory, but what's in a name?

For smaller additions and bay windows, you might want to choose lead as an appropriate roof covering, as it has the distinct advantage of shape: rolls can be formed over rounded timber battens running down the roof to allow the lead sheeting to be sized accordingly in bays and jointed. Lead for roof coverings like this is often of a greater thickness (and hence weight) than the lead used in gutters and flashings, and Code 6 or Code 7 is normally specified.

Gazebos

If your garden needs a focal point that a deck or patio alone can't provide, a gazebo could be the answer. Apart from adding height and structure to the garden, it can serve in summer as a functional building that can be used for eating outdoors, playing, or simply as a place to sit and enjoy the garden. Gazebos are often sold as DIY kits that are easy to assemble in a matter of hours, essentially an open-sided timber deck floor with posts supporting a solid roof. They can be square, but are frequently polygonal in plan.

Timber is the primary choice for gazebos, with cedar shingles for the pitched roof covering, but wrought iron in architectural swirls and Victorian elegance can make for a

grand and lasting building. In the case of the latter, aluminium pressed and profiled roof sheets are frequently used to give the impression of a greened copper roof. Other roofs may be thatched in Old English style for a country cottage appearance, or in African style for a more tropical beach feel.

By far the most economic roof finish is feather-edged boarding laid horizontally with the feathered edge uppermost and lapped as the boards progress up the roof to the apex. This is surprisingly effective, and if redwood or cedar is used it could last for some considerable time, particularly if the wood is kiln-dried. Even softwood, if it is factory-treated with preservative and of reasonable thickness, could last for many years.

Gazebos really only need a level site to set the base upon but I would strongly recommend forming a concrete base. Not only will this guarantee a permanently level base, but it will also help to spread the weight of the structure to the ground below, reducing the risk of subsidence.

As with all garden buildings, gazebos don't normally require permission of any kind, provided they aren't too tall: 4 m for a pitched roof and 3 m for a flat-roofed building are the limits; any taller, and you will have to seek Planning Consent. You should always check with your local planning department, particularly if you suspect that there is a public highway within 20 m, as this also has a bearing on its exemption.

Which materials?

The choice for any garden building is between buying it as a kit or whole from a specialist manufacturer, or having it purpose-built on site to your requirements. The suppliers often provide the labour to erect their products on site as an optional extra, and as they are experienced with the product, they are often quick and efficient. Garden buildings from DIY or garden stores remain of very low quality and can be overpriced; for a little more outlay, you can have something solidly built in timber frame that will last much longer.

It is possible to purchase quarried stone and have it carved into Corinthian columns, pilasters, copings and corbels. But most of us tend not to, and even when a stone orangery is required, what is mostly used today is parts made out of artificial 'reconstructed stone'. These mould-

formed architectural stone products are limestone-based, enabling a wide range of standard pieces to be catalogued. They aren't structural, but are intended to dress the front of a structure. Because of this they are perfect, variation-free, smooth-finished and completely absent of blemishes or imperfections – and because of this they look a little too perfect to have the true appearance of natural stone.

They are, however, a fraction of the price of stone, and the range of off-the-shelf and purpose-made products available is extensive. You could easily build an orangery from concrete blocks, and add a stone balustraded parapet wall, stone window and door surrounds and a couple of entrance pillars beside the French windows. With the walls rendered, it would look every inch authentic. That said, natural stone is pretty much reserved for flagstones and not much else in the 21st century, but an orangery or even a conservatory designed with these products creates an impressive and beautiful building.

CHAPTER THREE

Solving design problems

Overheating

In our lifetimes, UK residents haven't often been exposed to blisteringly hot weather – 'deprived of' would be a better phrase. Sunny days are often accompanied with cooling fresh breezes or cloudy intervals that keep the temperature down for most of the time, to the extent that we all rush towards a beach when we do get some heat. Because of this, we have been raised with a preconceived and well-founded view that for a garden to be successful it must be south-facing: to be enjoyed to the full, lawns, flowerbeds, patios and decks must capture the sun when it does appear by facing south.

Not surprisingly, we think of conservatories in the same vein, but in this case, quite wrongly. Indeed, if you could choose any orientation at

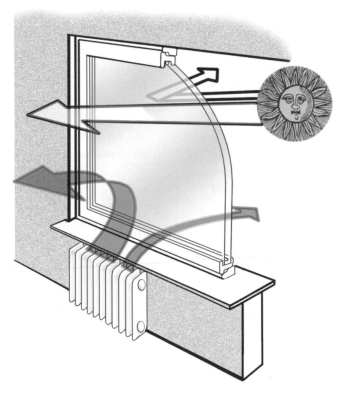

Conservatories can suffer from both excessive
heat loss and solar overheating

With glazed roofs and mostly glazed walls, both separation
from the home and shading are essential

all for a glazed roof to point, it would be east or west. Behind the glass a microclimate exists. With no cooling breeze and insulating glass reflecting the heat back in, the power of the sun is revealed all too frequently – and most of us fail to appreciate just how powerful that is.

The summer of 2003 was a rare reminder, with day after day of endless sunshine and regular high temperatures – on one notable day it even peaked at 38° C, setting a new record for a UK temperature. The life of some conservatory owners was not so grand that summer, and many glazed additions that were exposed to long hours of sun and heat were unusable for weeks on end.

During an earlier summer that was more typically British, I called on one such owner to view his conservatory, with the aim of discussing how it could be re-roofed in a solid-tile covered structure. He had explained over the phone earlier that he and his wife had been unable to spend much time in there beneath the polycarbonate because of the heat, and now they had tired of it completely. Could they convert it into a garden room with a pitched and tiled roof?

I think I arrived around mid-morning on what was a gorgeous day – no records were about to be broken, but it was very warm, and the owner was pleased that it was, as he could make his point. The lounge was pleasantly cool as he led me through, but he gave me the honour of opening the door to the conservatory, explaining that I'd appreciate it all the more.

You know that wall of heat that hits your face when you open the oven door to get the Sunday roast out? Well, it was like that – only the oven was bigger. I may have stepped back to check that my eyebrows were still attached. It was a furnace in there. Blinking to clear my watering eyes, I could see that the heat had been so great that the polycarbonate roof sheets had actually warped and buckled and could no longer be relied upon to keep the rain out. The upholstery of the armchairs had bleached, and the wallpaper (they had plastered and wallpapered the back wall) was peeling and bubbling off. We did the rest of the inspection from the outside.

I could see why they wanted to convert it, but it isn't easy trying to build a solid roof structure on top of a conservatory. The dead weight of the materials represents a considerable extra load, and with walls that are continuous window frames, there is nowhere to support it. PVC-u windows may have a little metal reinforcement inside them, but they aren't capable of bearing loads without lintels over the openings. In most conservatory building there are no lintels, and the lightweight roof sheets are taken to eaves beams that are supported by the window frames. The frames are side by side without any posts interspersing them – posts that could be used to support lintels – and the walls are too long for standard timbers or lintels to span along. In short, it isn't easy – not actually impossible, but jolly difficult and expensive to achieve, and most people faced with the task end up taking the framework of doors and windows down along with the roof and starting again.

So was there anything special about this conservatory that made it suitable for cooking a lamb joint in? Not really, it just had all those characteristics that tend to add to solar overheating and none, not one, of those attributes that help to avoid it. It wasn't just south-facing; it was south facing on a hill overlooking a valley without a garden tree or structure of any kind to spoil the view – exposed to the sun throughout the whole day. They had openable windows but left them locked shut all day, as they were both out at work, and no roof vents. And finally, they had no shading – they'd thought about it but concluded it would suffer the same fate as the furniture, and fitted blinds were too expensive to risk being damaged.

It has to be said at this point that blind manufacturers have risen to the challenge of conservatory overheating, and it is possible, if expensive, to have retractable blinds fitted to every section of the roof and every window. Some people have done this on south-facing conservatories, and although they all commented that it had cost almost as much as the conservatory itself, they considered it essential.

I think that with that splendid view, it must have seemed to the owners of the furnace that a conservatory to sit in and enjoy it would be perfect, and during the winter it might have been – if the roof hadn't been leaking.

Planning against overheating

Solar overheating is something you must consider at the outset – don't leave it to be a problem that you have to solve when you've finished.

It isn't difficult to sketch the basic shape of your home and garden on a piece of paper and endorse it with a compass point indicating north, at least magnetic north. Robbed of a compass, you can do worse than getting up early to see where the sun rises or consulting an Ordnance Survey map of your area – these maps are always drawn with north at the top and blessed with grid lines that also point south, east and west.

Don't despair if your chosen position faces due south, because there is more to be done yet. First, you may already have some shading existing in the form of a tree, shrubs or another building. The fact that deciduous trees increase in volume in summer with the production of leaves is a great advantage as a sunshade. On housing estates, other homes are often close enough to cast some shade at certain times of the day over your garden, and how much and at what times is something you can watch out for.

If you seem to lack any shade, you can build some in with tinted or bronzed roof sheeting that will dramatically shut down the amount of sunlight getting through. You can even buy reflective glass that that is made with a solar reflective coating to bounce back the radiation. You may have seen this used in commercial developments such as office buildings, whose windows take on a mirror quality.

Building in some permanent ventilation will be essential, and this needs to be secure enough to let you feel you can leave the home unattended with the vents open. Trickle vents on windows are the most secure of all. On an average window, however, they may only be 800 mm long and 10 mm wide, giving a cross-sectional area of 8,000 sq mm – not big enough to keep the room cool on a hot summer day, but with every window fitted with them, the cross-flow of air across the room will be enough for much of the time. In a room of 10 windows, 80,000 sq mm represents a hole the size of a basketball. Roof vents are effective as well, because heat rises and they offer it a place to escape out rather than build up.

The open-plan layout

One other solution to the problem of overheating is to look at opening up the conservatory to the home and letting some of that heat disperse around it. Given our love of daylight and the warmth of the sun, it seems crazy not to want the rest of your home to reap the benefits of a conservatory. Creating an opening in the wall between the two and making the conservatory an integral part of your living area changes many things, from the way you use the extra space to the regulations that apply and the impact they have. In fact, whether to separate your glazed addition with a door, or to open it to the home, is by far the biggest design question of all.

As we've already seen, even the highest standards of double-glazing fall dramatically short of what is required from insulation these days, and an extension with a glazed roof and mostly glazed walls is going to be far more sensitive to the outside temperature. In the UK, as in most temperate climates, we enjoy the possibility of a wide range of temperatures from well below freezing to well above 32° C, with record temperatures that wouldn't be out of place in the Sahara Desert. When the sun hits the glass, magnifying its power, high temperatures of 30° C can arrive in April and extend to the end of October, and even in the winter months it can exceed 20° C.

All of this means that an open-plan layout can benefit from the free heat of the sun and use it to centrally heat the air throughout your home, rather than build up inside the conservatory alone. In the cold, sunless days of winter, however, those long spells of icy winds and sub-zero temperatures will see your conservatory converted into a heat sink with a large unplugged hole in it. The warmth that your heating system is expensively creating to keep your home comfortable will be drained out through the opening to your glazed addition, leaving you struggling to keep the house warm and burning more and more energy to do so.

An insulating door or folding screen that allows you to close off the conservatory in cold weather and keep the heat in is a good idea, and not only that: since 1985 it has been essential in exempting conservatories from the Building Regulations. Indeed, without that insulating separation (which can be double-glazed itself) your conservatory needs to be controlled and approved under the Building Regulations. In the legislators' eyes, it is no longer an exempt conservatory but an extension to your home like any other extension, and this means that the stringent standards of thermal insulation that apply to the building of an extension relate to it. And sadly, that is often enough to kill the open-plan idea stone dead. Why? Because it simply isn't possible to meet those elemental standards of insulation for roofs using glass or polycarbonate. A more holistic approach is needed – one that looks at the home as a whole as it is at the moment and assesses how much heat is lost through it, and then looks at the proposed home with the open-plan conservatory added on and says, 'Is it really that bad?'

The answer to that question may determine whether approval is given for an open-plan design, or whether it must be separated and exempt from Building Regulations. To a large extent it is down to your local authority Building Control Officer and whether he or she will consider it to be reasonable. I am loath to get too technical on this matter, because one of us will struggle to keep up – and it may not be you – and both of us are likely to see our eyes glaze over. But since the open-plan conservatory succeeds or fails on this, it can't be avoided.

Calculating the heat lost from your home

It isn't difficult to calculate the amount of heat lost from any home, it is just a matter of measuring up the rooms and doing some simple arithmetic. It will help if you can prepare a simple sketch plan of each floor on which you can write down the dimensions. First, the ground floor needs to be measured and you can do this by adding up the area of each room on the ground floor that is heated. No need to measure upper floors unless they are over a garage or open space below. Similarly, only the outside walls and their window and door openings need to be measured and the areas of each recorded, not the internal walls, unless they separate a room from a garage or other unheated space.

The roof is where most of the heat leaves from, and its area should be measured. This is most easily achieved by using the floor area, if the roof is insulated at the ceiling level. If it's insulated at the sloping rafter level (as in a room-in-the-roof situation), the floor area on plan can be converted to the slope area by trigonometry or, in the absence of your school exercise books and a calculator with a cosine button, by using the factors below.

If you have different types of wall, window, door, floor and roof, the area for each type needs to be measured separately. For example, double-glazed windows and single-glazed windows or insulated cavity walls and solid walls: each type will have its own rate of heat loss, known as its U value, and this value needs to be established and multiplied to the area to work out the total heat lost from that element. U values can themselves be calculated precisely if you know the specification

ROOF PITCH	FACTOR
30°	plan area x 1.29
35°	plan area x 1.36
40°	plan area x 1.43
45°	plan area x 1.50
50°	plan area x 1.57

of your home's construction in great detail, but since most of us don't have that information, some typical U values are shown in the table opposite.

With the total heat loss from each element calculated, they can all be added together to reveal the total loss from your home as it stands today. Now all you have to do is add on the conservatory to the total, again using the proposed areas for it and the U values for each element (those for glass and polycarbonate are shown on pages 129 and 136). Don't forget to deduct from the original tally, the opening in the wall through to the conservatory.

Obviously there will be a larger amount of heat lost from the conservatory-extended home than from the existing home, but you can use both figures to show what the percentage increase in heat loss is.

If you're very lucky, you might have enough information at present to

TYPICAL U VALUES

Walls

Insulated	post-2002	0.35 U value
	1990–2002	0.45 U value
	1985–90	0.60 U value
Uninsulated	1976–85	1.00 U value
	pre-1976	1.60 U value

Roofs

Insulated two layers, between and over joists	0.16 U value
Insulated 200 mm thick one layer	0.25 U value
Insulated 100 mm thick one layer	0.40 U value

Floors

Insulated	post-2002	0.35 U value
	1990–2002	0.45 U value
Uninsulated		1.25 U value

convince your Building Control Officer that your proposals will only be adding a small percentage to the overall heat lost and answering the question 'Is it really that bad?' in your favour. It may be that you can add some insulation to your existing home to counteract the conservatory, reducing the percentage: extra loft insulation, replacement windows or cavity wall insulation are all worthwhile remedial measures.

If this isn't enough, the calculation could be extended further by calculating the conservatory extension with the 'notional'

HEAT LOSS

Some things will help you to achieve approval using total heat loss approach:

● An existing older home that has the scope to have its insulation improved.

● A large existing home

or

● A small proposed conservatory, either of which would mean the percentage of extra heat lost is kept small.

equivalent in an ordinary extension that complies with the insulation (U) values required. These values have been increasing periodically over the years, and you will need to check with your Building Control Officer what the current U values are. In this calculation you will be assessing what the heat loss would be if you built your conservatory to the same size but with the maximum allowed areas for windows and rooflights that a regular living area extension to your home would have. In 2004, for example, the guidance allows up to 25 per cent of the floor area in window area, and so you would calculate the total wall area of your addition and take one quarter of it as glazed to be multiplied by the required U value for glass and the rest for walls, multiplied by the minimum required U value for walls. In doing this you create an imaginary addition that is the worst in terms of thermal insulation that the regulations will allow you to build. You see where

we are going – you now have the information to compare your existing home as it stands today with the one you want to build (and the percentage of added heat loss), and the existing home and the one the Building Regulations would allow you to build.

The difference between those two percentage increases may now be small enough to convince your Building Control Officer that your proposal is reasonable. You can see that even a fully insulated normal extension is allowed some glazing for windows and doors, and will (simply because it makes the home bigger) be losing some extra heat anyway. In this respect, it might be necessary to reduce the size of your conservatory if you want it to be open-plan with your living space.

Where this approach is less convincing is where your home is relatively highly insulated already, such as a new home that can't be improved upon, and any conservatory addition will look bad in comparison.

If you fall into this category, your only hope may be to have an 'energy grade' produced for your home as extended and compare it to the energy grade on your existing home. For that you need a Standard Assessment Procedure, or SAP rating.

SAP ratings

All homes built since 1990 need a certificate that states what the carbon index is, a number between 1 and 10 that is a score on its energy efficiency, with 10 being the most efficient. Most homes built today would score in excess of 8. A surveyor who is qualified and authorised to calculate these ratings will be able to create one on paper based on your proposals, and since the calculation takes account of many detailed things in your home, including the heating and hot water system specification, the value is much more meaningful. Again it will show that your proposals will reduce the SAP rating – that much is inevitable – but the reduction may only be negligible and still show it to be high enough.

This is the important bit – you can build a new home today with an integral open-plan conservatory included in the design if you can show that the cardon index is at least 'x' amount. ('x' amount is prone to change, so you'll need to check its value now, but in 2004 it was 8.) So if your rating is at least this value, it will demonstrate that your home could have been built from scratch as you are now proposing, and that should clinch it.

If it doesn't, it might just be easier to retain an insulated door between the conservatory and keep it separate. When you think about it, the perfect solution might be to have a large opening fitted with folding doors that can be slid back on recessed floor and ceiling tracks to open the room up or kept closed to seal it off. If they are insulated, then you have answered the biggest design question with the word 'both'.

Insulation

The modern conservatory can be quite well insulated. The floor can be lagged beneath the screed or concrete, the cavity walls can be filled with insulation, the windows, doors and even the roof can be made to the highest specification of draughtproof double-glazing, all of which will reduce the rate at which heat escapes from the room. But this still can't compete with a solid roof lagged with glass fibre and walls that are more solid than glazed.

If you or your plumber thought you could solve the 'conservatory in winter' problem by installing bigger radiators in there, think a bit further. Heating a glazed room with fossil fuels, whether gas- or oil-fired central heating, electric radiators or solid fuel burners, leads to carbon being released into the atmosphere. Your

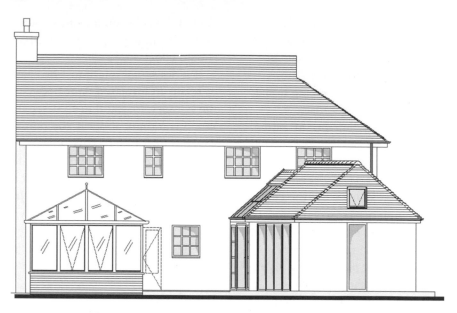

Garden room extension with a glazed link and a conservatory

Garden elevation of garden room and glazed link

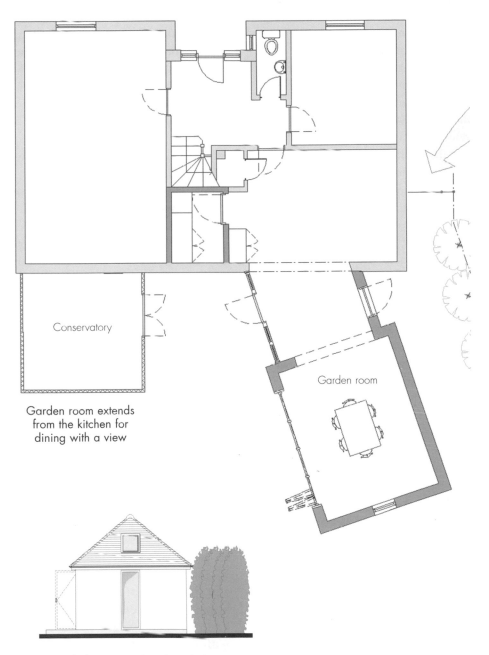

Conservatory

Garden room extends
from the kitchen for
dining with a view

Garden room

End elevation with reduced glazing

home is, of course, only a tiny source of carbon emissions, but collectively our homes make a more than generous contribution.

Mankind has been a little over generous with the amount of carbon it has released on the whole – 8,000,000,000,000 tonnes a year, which has meant that the natural cycle of carbon (the element vital for life) has been thrown into a bit of a wobble. It seems that nobody really knows what harm it will do to life in general, and indeed us, because as far as we are led to believe, it hasn't happened for nearly 500,000 years, and nobody was around then to witness it. However, all the indications are that it isn't good. The build-up of all this extra carbon in the atmosphere is trapping in the heat and slowly warming the planet. Maybe the oceans will come to our rescue or the plants, by dramatically increasing their carbon uptake to match our output, but then again, maybe not.

The point I'm eventually getting to is this: a glass extension has pros and cons, and the cons include insulation and the lack of it, which should be dealt with by design and not by the temptation to pump in further heat to make it habitable all year round. Even if you can afford the cost, the Earth might not be able to.

Controlled heating

If it can be achieved with little disruption to your home, extending the central heating system into this new room is the best way to provide heating there. Running a wet heating system into a semi-exposed room like a conservatory can attract some basic energy-efficiency measures, but nothing that doesn't make for good practice and cheaper fuel bills. If you think of your conservatory as a separate zone, you need to design in some ability to shut off the heating when you're not in there and control the amount of heat pumped in when you are.

These are two separate issues, both of which will allow you to control the heating in this vulnerable space.

First, plumbing in a flow bypass or loop will allow the conservatory part, the extended part, of the system to be closed off from the flow of hot water. Not only will the radiators be isolated from the supply of hot water, but the pipes serving them as well. A drain-off point on the system will allow this zone to be drained down when the room is unseasonally out of use; drain-off points are best located on the radiator tail pipe that is nearest to the external doors. To drain down this part of the system, a hose will have to be attached and the water run off to the outside. When this happens, having a nearby door is going to help and you should always make sure the water runs to a dead space or suitable drain – heating system water, treated with rust-inhibitor, will efficiently kill off grass and any other plants that it is discharged over, and by then your plumber will be gone, shrugging his shoulders somewhere else.

Second, controlling the temperature means introducing some thermostatic control. You can do this by way of thermostatic radiator valves or a programmable roomstat. Radiator valves known as TRVs have become standard equipment, but we tend to forget to alter them – left on a preset number and forgotten about, the control is gone, and before you know it, you'll be pumping heat from a piping hot radiator all week and never setting foot in there.

Much better is the programmable type of roomstat, which lets you set the room's minimum temperature as a separate zone and heats up the radiator only when it drops below that. Some models enable a different programme to be set for weekends than weekdays, and most allow three or more on-off settings per day. Your programme might keep a minimum night-time temperature of 10° C and a weekend daytime minimum of 16° C. If the sun comes out, the room temperature will soon respond very quickly, and so the heating system is really no more than a back-up in the event of solar failure, enough to keep the atmosphere and furnishings dry and the plants alive in winter.

Underfloor heating

With a low wall and a proliferation of windows in a conservatory, finding radiator space isn't always easy and many people choose underfloor heating simply to rid themselves of the clutter of pipes and radiators and allow total freedom with furnishings and decorating.

Instead of extending your central heating system with radiators to your new room, this allows you to use the whole floor as the radiator. Instead of a steel water-filled panel on the wall, an underfloor heating circuit consists of a loop of plastic pipes beneath the floor. The loop should have its own thermostatic control, so you can control the temperature of this separately to the rest of the system.

Under a solid ground floor, the pipes should be laid over insulation and pinned into it before being screeded over. Burying all that plastic pipework in cement and sand is a bit worrying, but the pipes are joint-free and pressure-tested before this happens, so there should only be a problem if you puncture the screed with fixings later on.

With timber floors, the pipes are supported in clips that also set the spacing of the loops and are fixed to the underside of the floorboards. 22 mm-thick flooring is required here to reduce the risk of the pipes being nailed through by carpet fitters.

If the water in your area is quite hard and limey, you should fit a limescale reducer to the supply; the in-line cartridge filled ones that require a new cartridge every 12 months are small enough to be plumbed in beneath a kitchen cupboard.

If you imagine the small surface area of even a double panel radiator heating a room, it needs to operate at a high temperature if it is to do its job. Underfloor heating is different: because the entire floor is your radiator, the temperature at which it operates is much lower, typically only 2° or 3° C above the room temperature required. In a sun lounge or a conservatory, maintaining heat to a relatively low background temperature at night should be much easier with this type of system. No longer will you be walking past a hot convecting current of air on one wall of the room; instead, the entire room is warmed gently and slowly to an even temperature. Conservatory floor finishes of tiles or stone are perfect for this form of heating; natural timber laminates and blocks are not ideal, given their thickness, but other forms of laminates can be used.

Condensation control

If you do plan to include plants to your list of fixtures and furnishings, you'll appreciate that in addition to absorbing carbon they have an ability to process it through photosynthesis and, in doing so, to release oxygen. The carbon cycle is something you don't notice going on outside, but indoors this process, combined with the moist soil that even pot plants need to flourish, can create a humid environment that without good ventilation will cause damp air and condensation. That's not a 'maybe', that's a 'will'. The glass will drip with it. It's more likely to occur when the temperature on the outside of the glass is much lower.

Even without plants, a not inconsiderable amount of water will have been used in the construction of the conservatory base and brick walls, and this will need to dry out over a period of time. Your average concrete base alone has well over a bathful of water in it, so give it a drying-out period before you bring in the soft furnishings, and if you can't leave the doors open to let it air, you could always hire a dehumidifier.

Another source of moisture that is often forgotten is trapped in the existing external wall that, now built over, has suddenly found itself to be an internal one. For the next 12 months it will slowly be coming to terms with this fact and gradually drying out. If you were thinking of laying carpet, don't until you're absolutely certain that the slab has totally dried out. The prospect of the damp being trapped beneath underlay will lead to what seems like a permanent musty smell and a damp quality you won't enjoy.

It isn't uncommon for the addition to be built off the kitchen (kitchens tend to be at the back of the house, exactly where most conservatories are added on), and kitchens have

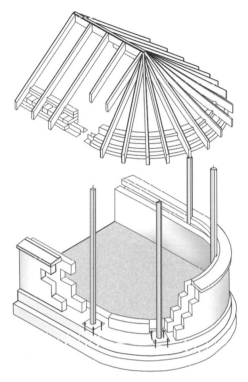

Spigotted posts support the lintel between glazing

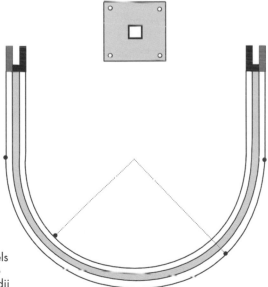

Semi-circular lintels
are available to
purpose-made radii

63

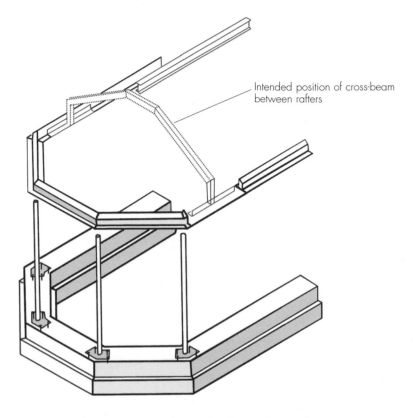

Intended position of cross-beam between rafters

A made-to-measure sun lounge lintel may also need a roof level cross-beam to tie the structure in

cookers and washing machines and tumble-dryers and bucketloads of moisture in the air. Cooking three meals a day, washing and drying clothes, plus dishwashing for the average family will produce something like 20 l of water every day, and if you've just covered the kitchen window with a conservatory, you can guess where all that water is going to condense.

It is best to ensure that all vents serving appliances are redirected to another external wall, even if that means doing some plumbing alterations or extending vent ducts through the conservatory to its adjacent outside wall.

You can also make sure that your kitchen has a mechanical extractor fan ducted to the outside air. If it's over a cooker in the form of an extractor hood, this is ideal. Kitchen extractors should have an extract rate of at least 60 l per minute, but many have variable speeds so you can turn them up when you are frying the chips. Do not be tempted to use a charcoal filter type instead, which might remove some of the smell but not the moisture. For a fan to work, it needs to be ducted over a shortish length of pipe and out through a sleeve in the wall. Some fans are described as centrifugal and some as co-axial; the former are most efficient.

Worse still is the idea of using a glazed addition to vent your appliances into, or, as some do, to use it as a utility room. All these are bad ideas unless you can ventilate the conservatory both permanently and rapidly. By 'permanently' I mean vents such as trickle vents and air bricks that are always open, as opposed to windows that are mostly shut. And by 'rapidly', I mean extractor ventilation and openable doors, roof and window vents. Even a conservatory can have an electrical extractor fan, which, fitted with a preset humidstat switch, can draw out the damp air. These humidstat models switch on the fan when the relative humidity of the air reaches a preset percentage – this is 65 per cent for bathrooms and kitchens, and if you choose a model that is adjustable you can increase this to a slightly higher setting to suit.

Designing in all these factors at the outset will help you to avoid the conversion problem later. If not, you could save yourself time and expense by incorporating the solid roof in your design now.

Sun lounges and garden rooms

The structural problems at the heart of all conservatory conversions still exist when building sun lounges from scratch, but here at least the supporting structure for a solid roof can be designed in from the outset, traditionally by installing an arrangement of lintels and posts raised from the dwarf walls to support the roof. Timber is the first material to consider for these elements, but it has the drawback of lacking strength in slenderness, so you need quite chunky section sizes to be able to use it. That's fine where it fits in with your design and the window frames can be set beside square posts 100–150 mm wide, but otherwise it can be tricky to accommodate them.

The alternative is to use steel, which has a greater strength that allows more slender sections to be used. Posts can be 50 mm square hollow sections or tubes sitting on baseplates that are fixed down to the walls and headplates that are fixed above to the lintels. Effectively you are building a series of goalposts here, with crossbar lintels in a structural frame to hold up the roof. Some lintel companies have taken advantage of the sun lounge problem and designed

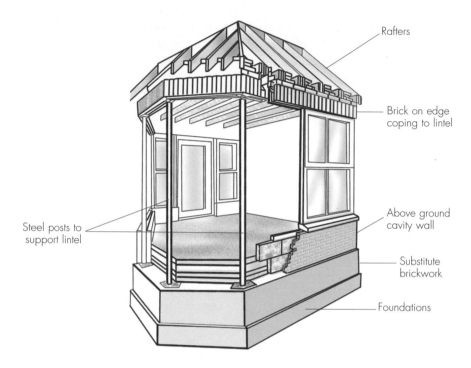

Rafters

Brick on edge coping to lintel

Above ground cavity wall

Substitute brickwork

Foundations

Steel posts to support lintel

Sun lounge designs can accommodate unsual shapes like the narrow hip-end

a series of standard lintels and posts, prefabricated for easy erection on site. They've had to establish a range of standard sizes for these models, but do have designs for hexagonal and even curved ends, retaining some of the best and most popular concepts in conservatory architecture.

The hexagonal model has a continuous ring beam lintel that is mitred at the corners and supported by posts that are spigotted in the factory for easy installation on site. The curved or bow-fronted models inevitably have a minimum radius

necessary for achieving the roof tiling and brickwork, but other, more simple designs, such as the standard bay window structure and built-in arches for circular or semicircular windows, are just as effective on smaller sun lounges.

You can achieve all this with your own steel fabricator and fixer, but the steelwork has to be treated against corrosion, and this is best done off-site. Factory-made lintels are made from galvanised steel, often with a zinc coating (usually of at least 600 g/sq m), and all the edges are treated.

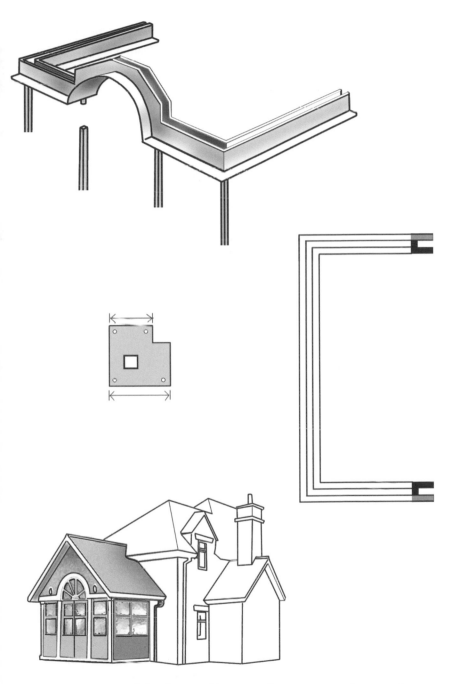

Using arch lintels can add a unique feature to a sun lounge entrance

Cutting up lintels and steel on site means that the exposed edges are vulnerable to rusting, and painting steelwork with red oxide or galvanising brush-on paint just isn't the same as having it factory-dipped in the stuff.

In the fight against oxygen and its corrosive effects, any additional treatment is worthwhile, and some lintel companies also powder-coat their products with a thermally set polyester coat. As steel is very badly behaved when it comes to thermal insulation, whenever possible lintel companies insulate the core of their shaped lintels with polystyrene to reduced the cold-bridging effect that lets the heat out. All things considered, I would use manufactured lintels and posts where your design allows you to.

As with any roof structure, these manufactured lintel and post arrangements rely on the roof being constructed to resist spreading; that is to say, it forms a triangle with ties (ceiling joists) joining the rafters together at their feet to restrain them. Without ties, the rafter feet will begin to make their own way out in the world and your roof will sag with their departure. If you were hoping to have a vaulted ceiling (or as Americans call it, a 'cathedral ceiling'), as conservatories do, you will need to include some tie beams. Again, preformed cradles of steel can be included and concealed between the rafters to tie the eaves

lintels via the ridge together. In this they have the advantage of achieving a totally uninterrupted ceiling space that can be plastered or boarded as you so desire.

If you want something to grow a vine over, you could always include a steel bar tying rod. Like those in conservatory design, the rods are threaded through the lintels and bolted to their outer faces, gathered beneath the ridge in a steel ring that also joins them to the ridge with a third stabilising bar. They are found in isolation in conservatory roofs, at least at far-apart centres, but remember that the solid roof represents a higher load and the spacing of these bar arrangements will be reduced. They can, with a few twists and some black paint, have a bit of architecture about them and tend to get used for the occasional hanging basket, appearing in this way to be more of an interior design feature than the reality of a structural intrusion.

Building near or on the boundary line

Any structure, conservatory or otherwise that is partly built against the boundary line or astride it, is covered by the Party Wall, Etc. Act 1996'. The words 'Don't panic' should be taken off the *Hitch Hiker's Guide to the Galaxy* and put on its cover. The Act is really just a procedure for homeowners to follow with their neighbours to avoid disputes.

Disputes over boundaries and walls are, you may not be surprised to hear, quite common, and this legislation was introduced to help avoid them, or at the very least keep them out of court.

The wall of your conservatory does not have to be a party wall for the Act to apply; it can just be on your side of the boundary facing on it. If they happen to have part of their home within 6 m of your new addition, additional measures will apply if you dig deep foundations that go beyond the depth of theirs. These measures are to avoid you robbing any structure next door of its support by digging out the ground through which it bears. You can rob support from a structure by digging near it, as opposed to directly beneath it.

Conservatory foundations are rarely deep, and these measures may not be necessary. More likely, with semi-detached and terraced homes, is the case of a single wall being built on the boundary, and for this you have a duty to notify your neighbour at least one month before you start work.

Strange as it may seem, to support a wall that is faced smack on the boundary line, your foundations may need to extend a bit over it, and the Act states that they have a legal right to do so. It also says that you will be responsible for any damage to your neighbour's property caused by the work and will have to compensate your neighbour accordingly if it happens. If you were planning on a reinforced raft foundation, be aware that the Act doesn't give you the right to place reinforced foundations on your neighbour's land, only traditional un-reinforced ones.

This notice should be in writing, and while you might discuss it informally, a signed document should pass hands as well – not just for now but for the future owners of either home. Unless you can fit 'Don't panic' on the envelope, you really ought to explain it to them, since few people have heard of the Act, and it can appear daunting if not threatening.

You can use the example notice on page 70 for this situation.

Unlike the other parts to the Act, which require a formal acknowledgement from your neighbour, this notice to build wholly on your own land up to the boundary doesn't need any response unless the foundations are reinforced, in which case they are described as 'special foundations' and a response is required. Use the draft acknowledge-ment letter shown overleaf to overcome any confusion if your neighbour is unsure how to respond.

To: Neighbour's name

Of: Neighbour's address

Date:

Dear............................,

Ref: The Party Wall, Etc. Act 1996

Proposed Conservatory – Line of Junction (Boundary) Notice

As the owner/s of (......your address.......) adjacent to your property (.......their address.......) I/we notify you of our proposal to build at the line of junction (boundary) between our properties.

This new wall, forming part of our conservatory/sun lounge, will be built wholly on my/our land up to the boundary line.

The proposed wall consists of (.......description of the wall and its materials. Facing bricks, concrete blocks, etc.......)

(Delete if not applicable)

Under the right given by section 1 (6) of the Party Wall, Etc. Act, it is intended to place projecting foundations partly under your land to support this wall.

(Delete if not applicable)

Under section 7 (4) of the Party Wall, Etc. Act, I/we wish to place with your written permission special (reinforced) foundations extending under your land.

I/We intend to start works on (.......date of commencement at least one month of notice.......), or with your written agreement on (.......date of commencement less than one month of notice.......).

In the event of any dispute between us under the Act, would you be willing to agree to the appointment of an independent Agreed Surveyor?

Yes/No

Name and address of Agreed Surveyor ....

Yours sincerely,

....

(print name and sign above)

THE PARTY WALL, ETC. ACT 1996
Acknowledgement of Notice

As adjoining owner/s under the Act of (... adjoining building's address...) and having received the notice/s dated .... in respect of the proposed conservatory/sun lounge at (...address of work...) and without prejudice to any of my rights under the Act,

I/We (.....name/s...) am/are

Content with the notice of at least one month

Content/not content for you to place special foundations projecting on our land

(delete entire sentence if not applicable)

Content/not content for you to start work on the earlier date of (...start date of less than one month...)

(delete entire sentence if not applicable)

In the event of a dispute arising under the Act, I agree to the appointment of an independent Surveyor (name and address to be agreed) to act as Agreed Surveyor between us if required.

Yours sincerely,

Signed...................................   Date..................................

Print name.....................................

CHAPTER FOUR

Planning Permission and Building Regulations

By far the majority of conservatories in England and Wales are exempt from Building Regulations approval, and many from Planning Permission.

Planning Permission

Conservatories, sun lounges and garden room extensions are all extensions to the home, and in planning terms aren't treated any differently to any other extension, which means that you have the same opportunity to avoid planning permission through Permitted Development (PD) rights. These rights give you the opportunity to extend your home up to a certain size without Planning Permission but there are conditions to them, and once they are used up, they are gone. So if you've already used your quota to extend, you can't use them again if this addition exceeds the limits.

The following is an overview of the exemption categories current in 2004. Because the law in this respect is prone to change, it should be considered only as a guide. For a full and definitive statement of the law, consultation should be made to the relevant and current statutory instrument at time of planning.

Planning Permission may or may not be required for your addition. A house which has not been extended before might still have PD rights. The law changes regularly as to what constitutes PD, and you should always check with your local Planning Authority for the current criteria and how your home and this proposal relate to it. Even if you don't need permission, it pays to get this fact in writing from them, either by letter or a Lawful Development Certificate. They will only do this on receipt of a letter accompanied by a detailed plan, and in some cases a fee. The plan should show the size of the addition and its position on your home, and should be fully dimensioned and not simply drawn to scale.

Under the Town and Country Planning Act 1990 (General Development Order), current guidelines for Permitted Development of Domestic Additions in England and Wales are as follows (variations in Scotland under the Town and Country Planning (General Permitted Development) (Scotland) Order 1992 are shown in brackets).

Ground-level additions (conservatory, garden room, sun lounge, etc.) which are:

● No higher than the highest part of the existing roof

or:

- When it is within 2 m of your property boundary it is in no part higher than 4 m.

- Adding less than 50 cu m to the volume of your home.

General cases
Upper-level additions (conservatory, sun lounge, etc.) to the roof in which:

- The addition will add less than 50 cu m to the volume of your house.

- The addition is to a roof slope that does not face the highway.

- The addition does not increase the height of the roof.

Special cases
are terraced houses and also properties in the following designated areas: Area of Outstanding Natural Beauty, National Park, Conservation Area, Norfolk and Suffolk Broads.

- The addition is no bigger than 10 per cent of the existing house (including the roof) in volume (Scotland – in floor area) or 50 cu m* (Scotland – 16 sq m floor area) (whichever is the greater) and definitely no bigger than 115 cu m* in volume (Scotland – 30 sq m floor area).

- An addition to the roof such as a dormer window is only exempt in the case of terraced houses if it is no bigger than 40 cu m* in volume.

NOTE: In the other special areas listed above, Planning Permission will be required.

* In all cases volume is measured externally and includes roof space.

- That no part of your addition is nearer to a public highway than any part of the existing house unless it is at least 20 m away from your finished house (as extended).

- There are no permitted development rights for additions to or in the grounds of Listed Buildings. Listed Building Consent will be needed.

- No Article 4 directive is in force on your property or the Permitted Development rights have been removed (they are sometimes in Conservation Areas, on new housing developments or contaminated sites where greater control is needed for some reason or another.)

Some facts worth noting:

- Conservation Areas are defined as 'areas of special architectural or historic interest, the character or appearance of which it is desirable to preserve or enhance.' They are designated by the local authority in consultation with parish councils, local amenity societies and the general public. Developers can be a little remiss in pointing out to new home owners that they have no PD rights imposed by the development's Planning Permission. It could after all devalue a property in some people's eyes. The information will be included on the deeds to your home, but you should check with the planning department as to the detail. If PD rights have been removed, it could mean that you need Planning Permission to erect anything from a fence or a garden shed upwards.

- Areas of Special Control exist in some parts of the UK, which, although too small to be considered as Conservation Areas, have been designated so to protect their architectural or historical value. Permitted Development will be affected.

- Farmhouses are not usually considered as Domestic Dwellings for planning purposes.

- Additions to council houses will also require the permission of the local authority Housing Department. Even subsequently bought council houses may carry restrictive covenants to this effect.

Because the first Town and Country Planning Act came in on 1 July 1948, anything built on or after that date in the way of extensions, porches, garages, etc. counts towards your permitted development quota, and if your property has had any add-ons since 1 July 1948, you might not have any PD rights left at all. If this is the case, you may only recover PD by demolishing some or all of the old buildings in the same category.

In England and Wales, the local planning authority will notify your neighbours of your proposals either by letter, advertisement in the local press or a notice displayed nearby. In Scotland, it is your responsibility as the applicant to consult the neighbours and submit their signed comments to the Planning Department. Forms for this purpose are usually acquired with the Planning Application forms and should be returned completed when the application is made. In the former, interested parties have a couple of weeks to lodge their objections if they have any. It is therefore sometimes beneficial to show them your plans and consult with them beforehand.

Many people and organisations are consulted in the planning process – parish councils, environmental groups, etc. – and it takes some time for all comments to be collected. If there are any objections, it does not necessarily mean that your addition will be refused. It does mean that it will be presented at a planning committee or sub-committee meeting and will thus be decided by elected councillors rather than by delegated powers (i.e. by Planning Officers). In reality, the case officer will prepare a short report and make a recommendation, which more often than not will be adopted. You should be entitled to see any such report together with any consultees' comments, but you will not be sent them automatically, so make enquiries and ask.

In Northern Ireland, planning applications are made to the Department of the Environment for Northern Ireland, who have six divisional offices. These offices carry out the planning function in place of the local authorities, although they do consult with them.

Planning Approval is likely to be given with conditions. One condition is likely to be that work must start within five years, or the approval becomes invalid and you will have to make another application. Another condition may be that samples of materials must be submitted for approval or matched with existing ones before work starts.

Planning Authorities must have a good reason for refusing permission. The assumption should always be one in favour of an application and not against it.

Refused Planning Permission

In the event of your application being refused Planning Permission, try to establish from your Planning Officer what the exact nature of the objection was. The reasons should be printed on the refusal notice, but they are likely to be in planning jargon with policy references, so try to discuss ways with your Planning Officer as to how they could be overcome by revising the scheme. If this isn't possible, your only other recourse is to submit a Planning Appeal to the Secretary of State, Department of the Environment, Transport and the Regions (or the Welsh Office, Scottish Office or DOE for Northern Ireland as appropriate).

Currently appeals are a lengthy and time-consuming process. Often after the appeal is submitted it takes four to five months before the inspector visits the site, and then another two to three months after the visit before a decision is issued. The Planning Inspectorate do not currently charge for appeals, so an appeal can be entirely free if you do it yourself. Many people engage their solicitor in this process, but frankly, if they are not fully conversant with local planning policies and government advice circulars (and most won't be), they are likely to be only of administrative help. Planning Consultants who specialise in planning applications and appeals

PLANNING APPEAL TIMETABLE

Two weeks after receiving the appeal, the council will send you a questionnaire they have completed, and they will notify those who objected before. After six weeks, written reports will be submitted to the inspectorate by yourself and the local authority, giving your reasons for appealing and theirs for the refusal.

The inspectorate will forward copies to all involved parties, so you don't have to notify them.

After nine weeks, you can comment on their report and contest any new issues or points that have been raised that weren't covered before.

You then wait for the inspectorate to notify you of a site visit date. At the visit, you are able to point out features raised in the appeal so that they aren't missed, but you are not permitted to discuss the reason for appealing or argue over the reasons for refusal. If the site can be seen from public land (the road for example), the inspector may visit unaccompanied.

are the best choice, but their fees may not be proportional to the benefits, so have a long and careful think before engaging one. Appeals may also be made against conditions of approval if you consider them to be unacceptable.

You can also appeal against the Planning Authority's failure to give you a decision on your application inside eight weeks. Not many people do, because it can take the best part of a year to get a Planning Appeal decided, by which time you might as well have waited for the council to make the decision.

If you do decide to appeal against refusal, you have to lodge the appeal within three months of the refusal date; not just the forms, but all the accompanying documents that go with them.

The appeal would normally be dealt with on the basis of a written statement in which you may quote the case for your application to be approved, and request that the council's decision is overturned. Although the written procedure is essentially about preparing a text argument, you can illustrate it with photographs and drawings if they serve a purpose.

The application may have been refused on a design basis, or it may be a fundamental refusal of the principle of adding anything on to the home; either way, you will need to know what it is you are appealing against. Anyone who objected to your Planning Application will be notified of the appeal by the local authority, and they will have an opportunity to comment again to the inspectorate if they wish.

Bear in mind that planning inspectors have complete freedom of judgement in considering your appeal and can, in deciding, make matters worse for you. For example, your conservatory application was refused because of the proposed boundary elevation windows that would overlook next door, which you could have redesigned as a solid wall to gain approval. Instead, you lodge an appeal, and the inspector finds not just against the boundary windows but against the whole conservatory. What was a minor redressable situation is now a major lost one.

Complaints can be made to the Local Authority Ombudsman if you consider that the local planning authority has been guilty of maladministration regarding your application. This means that you believe they have mishandled the planning process, and in doing so jeopardised your application's chances of success. In other words, it is not the decision that is important in this instance, but the way in which it was reached. Local authorities have a duty to follow legislative procedures in processing Planning Applications, and such a complaint can only be successful it can be proved that they have neglected those procedures to your detriment. A lot of complaints to the Ombudsman are thrown out as having 'no case to answer' simply because the appellant has not understood this fact and is simply objecting to the council's decision, i.e. the refusal.

Planning considerations include:

Overlooking

If your addition includes windows that overlook a neighbouring property, the Planning Officer may consider that in doing so they encroach upon the privacy of the people living there.

It is usually not sufficient to suggest glazing this side with obscure glass unless it is structural glazing (such as glass blocks), as it is relatively simple for future owners to replace the glass in standard windows with a clear pane. Apart from removing the windows entirely and replacing them with a wall, the only other solution is to design them as high-level windows with the bottom cill height at least 1.78 m above the finished floor level.

Design

The visual appearance of the addition is a prime consideration and one which is often the cause of much disagreement. Clearly 'good design' is a matter of opinion, and some Planning Officers have been known to disagree with home-owners as to what constitutes it. Some design choices for conservatories are looked at on page 31.

Scale

This is also important and may relate as much to the amount of available room in your garden as to the impact on the existing property, and indeed the neighbourhood. If the addition is too big, the Planning Officer may consider your proposal to be overdevelopment.

Home office space

If your addition is aimed at providing you with a home office, you do not necessarily need Planning Permission to change from dwelling to business use, providing that your home remains principally your home – a place of private residence. It is only

a change of use, when either the majority of the property is given over to offices or when a number of employees, in addition to yourself, work on the premises. Starting a business from a conservatory on the side of your home will have limitations in both practical and Building Regulation terms, but as far as planning goes you'll be fine, so long as it doesn't grow into an office with employees. I mention this because, with more of us working from home, for at least part of the time, a conservatory or sun lounge can make for additional and valued space at a budget price. And because every so often an architect or, more often, a solicitor thinks that moving in a bank of filing cabinets, plus draughtsmen or secretaries, to a conservatory on their home is a really neat idea.

If your starter business is starting with only you, be prepared to apply for both Planning Permission and Building Regulations Approval when it grows to more.

Listed Building Permission

If you live in a Listed Building, you will need to apply separately for Listed Building Consent, even if your addition does not require a Planning Application.

The good news is that currently no fee is paid for Listed Building Consent applications, where ordinary ones are charged around £115 (in 2004) and go up frequently. The work is zero-rated for VAT purposes, and you should be able to recover the VAT paid on all materials. Labour shouldn't be charged with VAT in the first place if you've advised your builders that it is a Listed Building.

Listed Buildings are found throughout the United Kingdom: your local planning authority will have a copy of the list for their area, should you need to check. Not an inconsiderable amount of design detail may be necessary, such as large-scale details of the frame joinery and glazing bars.

Building Regulations

The vast majority of conservatories built in England, Wales and Northern Ireland are exempt from complying with the Building Regulations. Scotland, where the exemption criteria has been much more onerous, can't be included in this statement.

The Building Regulations impose health and safety, energy conservation and accessibility requirements onto the built environment, and provided you meet these minimum standards in the design and construction of any controlled addition, you will receive Building Regulation Approval. In Scotland, approval is given in the form of a Building Warrant.

If you have any doubts as to the exemption criteria and how they relate to your proposal, phone or visit your Building Control Officer, who will be only too pleased to discuss matters with you. Most will have Exempt Enquiry application forms that you can obtain and complete for a written confirmation of exemption. As with Planning, it is worth obtaining these to avoid future problems with conveyancing.

Exempt Criteria for Conservatories

Building Regulations 2000 (as amended) England and Wales Building Regulations (Northern Ireland) 2000

The exemption categories that include conservatories are described below:

Extensions to buildings at ground level only comprising

● A conservatory, porch, covered yard or covered way no greater than 30 sq m internal floor area, are exempt if the glazing meets the requirements of Part N (Building Regulations 2000) or Part V (Building Regulations (Northern Ireland) 2000)

Part N is the approved document in England and Wales (Part V in Northern Ireland) that gives advice on the use of safety glass in critical locations, so conservatories are only exempt if safety glass is used in these critical zones. If it isn't, an application is required and the Building Control Officer will require you to use safety glass in theses areas. I know it's weird, but it's the way the legislation works – by the way, safety glass is necessary in case you were thinking of building something entirely with horticultural glass, greenhouse style.

A definition of a conservatory for exemption hasn't been published in England and Wales. The Government's legal definition of a Conservatory (when pressed) is hopelessly out of date. Building Control Offices throughout the land have tried to expand on the exemption conditions within the spirit of the regulations. Needless to say, these unofficial conditions can vary somewhat from place to place, and so it is imperative that you seek the views of your local Building Control Office before proceeding.

An example of what is currently viewed as necessary in some regions includes:

- Should be used seasonally and not for year-round occupation.

- Should in some part be used for plants.

- Should in part have a translucent roof.

- Separation from the remaining habitable parts of the home, by a wall, partition or door. Fully glazed doors would be OK if they were double-glazed, but might not be if only single-glazed.

- No fixed heating should be installed, or if it is, it should be capable of being isolated from the rest of the home. An electric radiator that can be switched off or thermostatically controlled might be no problem, but extending a wet heating system out there could induce extra requirements. This could mean just having to fit a thermostatic radiator valve or roomstat with a frost setting so that it can be shut down in winter, or it could mean installing a loop in the central heating system that can divert hot water away from the room altogether, so that no water pipes within the conservatory are in use when the flow is diverted.

These measures, which are aimed at energy efficiency and reducing carbon emissions, may or may not apply where you live, and even if they do, it might be possible to design your way through them satisfactorily.

To the best of my knowledge there are no Building Control Officers checking completed conservatories for the presence of tender plants or seed propagation, but you never know: I expect that somewhere, somebody is following the law to the letter.

The Northern Ireland Building Regulations have a general definition of a Conservatory: 'Conservatory means a part or extension of a building attached to and having a door giving access from the attached building and having not less than three-quarters of the area of its roof and not less than one-half of the area of its external walls made of translucent material.'

Regulations always lack punctuation, and it's important to breathe correctly if you're going to read them out loud, but at least they have a definition and everyone in Northern Ireland knows what a conservatory is. If yours doesn't fit this description, it can't fall into the exemption category, regardless of its size.

Building Regulations 1990 (as amended) Scotland
Part II Buildings attached to Dwellings (excluding Flats and Maisonettes)

● Conservatories that are glazed to meet the safety glazing requirements and have a floor area up to 8 sq m

And do not contain

● Sanitary accommodation

● A combustion appliance (e.g. a boiler, Aga, solid fuel, oil or gas fire) or a flue

And are not located

● Within 1 m of your boundary

● On land within the boundaries of which there are harmful or dangerous substances (i.e. contamination).

Note that in all cases, for conservatories to be exempt they must be glazed with safety glass, such as laminated or toughened in all critical locations, which are described on page 39.

● If you do plan to fit a fire or boiler, you should seek advice regarding the ventilation and flue required to serve it. An application for Building Regulation approval or a warrant in Scotland may be necessary for a 'controlled fitting'.

Not exempt?
If your proposed addition doesn't fit the exemption criteria, you will need to comply with the Building Regulations and submit an application to them. This can take one of two forms, full plans or a building notice, either of which must be submitted before you start work.

Applying for Full Plans Approval

This is what it says on the tin. The plans are full and detailed in technical specification, and are vetted and approved. If any amendments or additional information is needed, the officer will write to you in this respect or impose them as conditions of the approval. If they are deficient to the extreme in information or contravene the regulations, they will be rejected. If you are using a specialist conservatory supplier, they usually have technical drawings that can be supplied to you for full plans applications.

A Rejection Notice for Building Regulations may be overcome by redesigned-presenting the plans suitably amended and completing the application forms again; no extra fee is required for a straight resubmission.

Rejection of plans and determinations

Because the requirements of the Regulations are functional requirements, there is some scope for deciding what constitutes compliance and what doesn't. The scope is reduced by the Approved Documents, which give detailed advice on all the requirements, but they aren't intended to be the sole means of showing compliance.

If you feel your design has been unjustly refused based on these or any other standards or accepted

THE STAGES FOR NOTIFICATION USUALLY INCLUDE:

1. Commencement	2 days notice
2. Foundation excavation	1 day notice
3. Foundation concrete	1 day notice
4. Oversite preparation	1 day notice
5. Damp-proof course	1 day notice
6. Drains before covering	1 day notice
7. Drains testing	1 day notice
8. Occupation	1 day notice
9. Completion	2 days notice

guides, such as British or European Standards and BBA (British Board of Agrement) certificates, you can appeal to the Office of the Deputy Prime Minister for a determination. As with a Planning Appeal, the ODPM will consider both sides of the argument and make an informed decision on which to support in a written determination – a judgement, if you like, as a referee, and a legally binding one. You can only use this procedure at the design stage on a refused Full Plans Application. It is not possible to use it when the work is in progress. As with Planning Appeals, it can be a long, long time before the determination is given, so you need to care enough about your design to leave it for a year or so before starting work.

It's worth knowing that the Government has in the past given determinations on conservatory design, in particular one on an open-plan design that failed to demonstrate compliance with the insulation standards of the Regulations. Here, they took the view that the proposal was an extension and not a separated conservatory, and as such it should meet the standards in respect of energy conservation imposed on extensions. The determination was not successful in that instance. Details of determinations can be found on the Department's web site.

Advice on Building Regulations

If you need any advice on particular requirements of the Building Regulations, the Building Control Section of your local authority will be able to help. In England and Wales the requirements are contained in 'Approved Documents' lettered A to P issued by the ODPM as guides. In Scotland, there are currently 17, parts A to T. (Parts I and O don't exist.)

Each one deals with separate issues: in England and Wales, Part A – Structure, Part B – Fire Spread, Part C – Resistance to Weather and Ground Moisture. Approved Document L comes in two parts, the first, L1, for dwellings and the second, L2, for other buildings – these are the guides for energy conservation, and they are thick. The same system exists in Northern Ireland and Scotland, but in each of these cases the Parts are lettered differently.

The Approved Documents can be purchased from HMSO or any good bookshop, and have recently been published on CD-ROM. You are not going to need to buy them for one addition, but if you do need to refer to them, they are usually found in the reference section of public libraries and at your local authority Building Control Office.

Most people have some idea of what they want their addition to provide, and instruct their designer accordingly. Often 'plan-drawers' will simply draw up what the customer requires without offering any advice at all, so if you do go for an architect-designed addition, make sure you get a worthwhile design service.

Building Control on site

It is a requirement of the Building Regulations that you or your builder notifies the Building Control Officer at various stages of the work, and leaves the work at these stages exposed for inspection before covering it up and continuing. Failure to give such notice may mean that you are required to break open and expose the work for inspection later.

Notice should be in writing, and most authorities provide cards that can be used for this purpose. A fax is an excellent way of giving notice, since it endorses the request with the time and date it is transmitted. Some authorities may operate a telephoned or e-mail notice system. If you don't receive an inspection within the time limit, it is extremely unwise to carry on without first contacting the Building Control Office to check why they haven't come out, and to give them an 11th-hour opportunity to do so.

Building Control Officers do not supervise the work on your behalf. They carry out spot checks to see that the minimum standards of the Building Regulations have been met. If you are in any doubt as to the quality of workmanship your builder will apply, you should appoint your own surveyor to oversee the project. A private surveyor can ensure quality control of the work, authorising stage payments as the job proceeds.

Completion Certificates

These certificates are evidence that your work complied with the requirements of the Building Regulations in its construction.

Once the work is finished, a Completion Certificate should be sought from your Building Control Office. This is a valuable piece of paper which will be required should you sell the property or redesigned-mortgage it in the future. It is a statement that the work complies with the Building Regulations. Until

now, you may only have a Plans Approval notice that says that your plans comply.

What if you or a previous owner has built an addition without getting the necessary permissions?
First, check to see if permission was needed. There are procedures for correcting unauthorised work if it wasn't done too long ago.

Lets deal with Planning Permission first. If you've discovered that the addition should have had Planning Permission and didn't, it is usually a case of making a normal application retrospectively. If the planning authority decides that the work isn't acceptable and breaches planning controls, they will refuse permission. Normally this would mean that you would be advised formally of the reasons for refusing it, and also on what measures you need to take to remedy the breach. They would fix a date by which this corrective work would need to be completed.

They may implement this enforcement by way of a condition imposed on your Planning Permission, or they may refuse permission and serve an enforcement notice. Conditions of approvals are enforceable, and if you don't meet them the authority has the power to serve a Breach Of Condition Notice on you.

As with normal applications, you have the right to appeal against an enforcement notice if you wish to. Until the appeal is decided by the Secretary of State, the notice is suspended and unenforceable.

With regard to a Breach of Condition Notice, there is no right of appeal and you run the risk of prosecution if you fail to comply with it. It is, however, possible to apply to the planning authority itself to have a condition removed.

For detailed advice on how to appeal against enforcement notices, contact your local planning authority or the Planning Inspectorate.

Building Regulations have been in their current format of 'functional requirements' with guidance notes (Approved Documents) since November 1985, and if the work was done after then and doesn't meet the exemption criteria, you are eligible to apply for a Regularisation Certificate. This is retrospective approval and is not available for any additions built before this date, before which, incidentally, conservatories were less frequently exempt.

The fee you pay is slightly more than the standard fee (120 per cent of it), but you do not have to pay VAT on it. Alas, it is usually not as easy as paying a fee and waiting for the certificate to arrive. The Building Control Officer will have to inspect the work done, and this could mean exposing parts of the construction. The officer will need to assess the structural design of the addition, and you might be required to provide structural calculations and details justifying this element. Weather resistance, insulation and ventilation will also be on the list of things to check out, together with the all-important fire safety issues. Whatever the requirements were at the time the work was executed will apply now, and it is quite likely that you will have some corrective or additional work to do to bring the addition up to scratch.

If the problem is simply that the door has been absent between the home and the conservatory, leaving it open-plan it may just be a case of blocking up the opening and installing a door to a suitably insulating standard. Once this is done and the officer is happy that the work either complies or is exempt, a Regularisation Certificate or letter will be issued, and you should keep this with the property deeds – it will prove invaluable should you ever sell or remortgage your home.

Leaving it as unauthorised is not a good idea. For one thing, it may represent a threat to the health and safety of your family and visitors. For another, you will find it difficult if not impossible to sell the home or remortgage it when you want to.

CHAPTER FIVE

Base

Most but not all conservatories will sit quite happily on a simple concrete slab base that will serve as both foundation and floor structure. Some ground conditions will make conventional foundations much more suitable. If the ground is covered by a deep layer of topsoil or imported earth (also known as backfill material), it will be far better to dig trench foundations down into the natural subsoil as you would with a conventional extension or new building.

Of course, even with foundations under your walls you will still need to support the floor slab on a sound base, and the construction of a conservatory is no different to this. Ground-bearing bases are usually in the region of 100 mm thick and are cast over a level bed of hardcore known as the oversite. In essence, they are the standard ground-floor construction of modern homes. Where no foundations occur beneath the walls, the slab base is extended out beneath the walls to support both them and the roof.

For the concrete base to function properly in either role it must be carefully formed, and there are several key elements to its design and construction. The following key points will help you to ensure a good concrete base.

Levels

Ensure that all the vegetation is dug out and removed, along with any topsoil, and begin from your calculated formation level on the subsoil. If you need to match up with the finished floor level between your home and the addition, it is vital to correctly calculate the depth of construction. Mark the level of your floor finishes on the existing external wall and measure down from this the layers of your base construction before filling with the oversite material. This should make sure that you don't overfill and end up with too little thickness of concrete, or under fill and end up needing too much.

50 mm floor screed +
100 mm concrete base +
50 mm insulation +
250 mm oversite and blinding +
= 450 mm total depth of construction

Oversite material

Casting the concrete directly on the ground is rarely possible (one exception could be where solid chalk subsoil is present and it can be bladed flat to the level required). So that the quality of the preparation beneath it

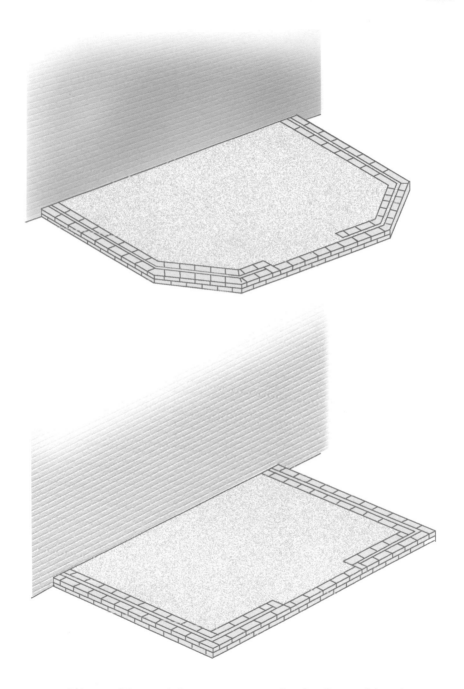

A simple base will be needed to support even a dwarf wall around the edge

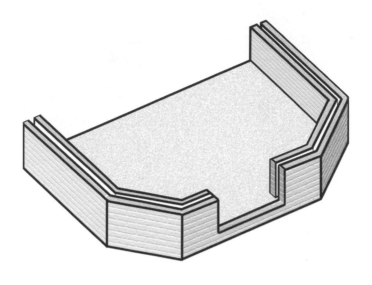

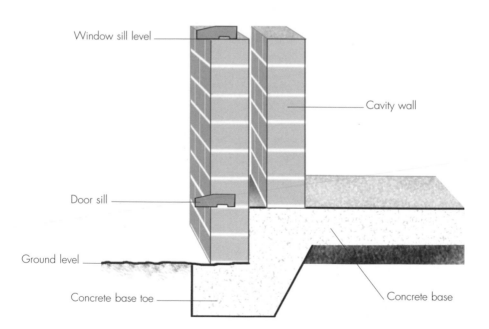

Window sill level

Cavity wall

Door sill

Ground level

Concrete base toe

Concrete base

This cross-section shows how the edge of the base can be formed with a toe to support the outer skin of facing bricks

GOOD OVERSITE MATERIAL	BAD OVERSITE MATERIAL
Clean broken bricks, concrete,	Earth
broken paving slabs or roof tiles	Soft insulating blocks
Reject or crushed stone (washed)	Poor-quality demolition rubble
Type 1 or type 2 graded stone	Road scrapings
Crushed concrete fines	Deep sand
	Colliery shale

can determine how long it lasts, the hardcore material should be no larger than 100 mm (half-brick) units.

Depth of oversite

The oversite material must be at least 150 mm thick and can't simply be dusted over the ground, but where it becomes a greater problem is when it's too deep. The limit for ground-bearing bases is 600 mm, since it is likely to settle and cause cracking if it is much deeper. If part of it exceeds 600 mm deep, it is best to use lean-mix concrete in layers with the hardcore to make up the difference, or a type of stone fill, such as 40 mm pebble stone, that cannot settle. Like a bag of marbles, once the substructure walls are filled with stone-type fill and it has been compacted to the subsoil at the bottom, there it remains. It is therefore ideal for deep-fill floor slabs.

Compaction

Ensure that the hardcore is compacted in layers no more than 225 mm thick, ideally mechanically compacted with a plate compactor. Take care not to push out the external walls where a stone type fill is used.

Blinding

The hardcore should be finished off with a blinding of fine material such as sand to a maximum thickness of 20 mm. Do not lay the blinding material too thick. It is only intended to protect the polythene damp-proof membrane from being punctured by sharp edges of hardcore, and you shouldn't sink into it when walking on it.

Damp-proofing

Most damp-proofing is done beneath the concrete slab by laying a polythene damp-proof membrane

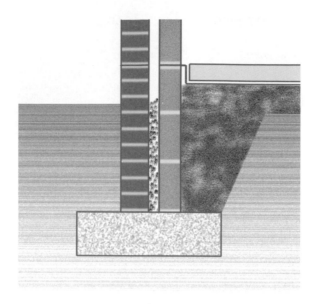

Strip foundation

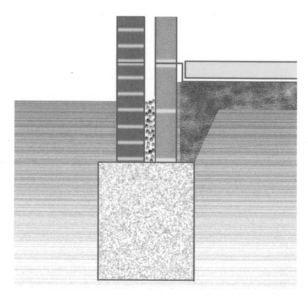

Deep strip or trenchfill foundation

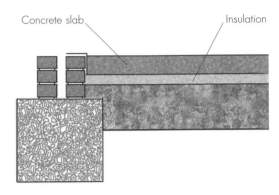

Concrete slab   Insulation

Insulated floor slab

(DPM). If it isn't in one piece, it should be lapped and the joints taped down, and where separate foundations have been formed, ensure that it is dressed up the outside walls so it can be trimmed back after concreting. The DPM can help to protect the concrete slab from sulphate attack, but since sulphates may be contained in some fill material, such as brick rubble, it's a good idea to use polythene beneath concrete generally.

Insulation

To keep some of the cherished heat in, the base should also be insulated, and it's important to use the correct type of insulation graded for floors and not walls.

Polyurethane foam board is often used in 50 mm thickness or more. If you have separate foundations for the dwarf walls, thinner strips (25 mm) can be cut to stand it up the sides of walls to the slab depth when insulating below the concrete slab, so that it is cast fully encased.

While floor-grade insulation can be laid beneath the concrete, there are advantages in it being placed later on top of the concrete beneath the finishings and if you have a simple slab base with no separate foundations, this is your only option. It reduces the time taken to warm up the floor structure if you aren't trying to heat 100 mm of concrete slab as well. The advantage of having it beneath the concrete is that the base will store heat through the day and release it at night, but only where it is fully encased and separate foundations are used.

91

Avoiding cracks

Make sure you are not forming the hardcore on backfilled or contaminated ground, or indeed settlement, as clay shrinkage or heave will cause problems. Even on good subsoil, the addition of lightweight fabric reinforcement such as A142 is beneficial in avoiding settlement cracks.

In very large bases, movement joints such as fibrous material strips should be used to allow some expansion to occur without damaging the slab.

- There are sound environmental reasons for reusing demolition hardcore in oversite preparations, but it is essential that it is handpicked and 'clean'. Be prepared to spend some time sifting the rubbish out if you're using demolition material.

- Note that sulphates in hardcore or in subsoil can attack concrete. Where this is likely, you should use sulphate-resisting cement in lieu of ordinary Portland cement (OPC), Polythene DPMs will also help to resist sulphate attack, and should always be included beneath any concrete base to resist damp. The industry standard grade for polythene in this use is 1200 gauge, and you can check the wrapper of any supply to establish it – more often than not, it is coloured blue or black. Polythene is available in much thinner gauges for all manner of different uses from dust sheets and vapour checks upwards, and so it isn't difficult for unscrupulous builders trying to save a few pounds to install a substandard grade here. The risk is that polythene is easily punctured by concrete poured over it, or if the hardcore on which it lies isn't of a suitable and durable thickness.

> **DIY CONCRETE MIX FOR GROUND-BEARING SLABS:**
>
> 25 kg (0.0175 cu m) of cement to
>
> 0.05 cu m of building sand to
>
> 0.1 cu m of coarse aggregate.
>
> (or 10 x 25 kg bags of cement to every
>
> 1 cu m of all-in ballast)

Base finishing

The concrete of the base is normally tamped with a timber beam to a level finish that can be screeded over later, unless you require a smooth finish either to be left exposed or covered by a floating finishing.

A floating floor finish is any finishing layer that isn't bonded or fixed down to the concrete base or structure. Laminate and timber floors are often just laid over the insulation

SOME POINTS TO CHECK IN BASES FOR FLOATING FLOORS

● Ensure that the insulation is laid perfectly flat and level on the concrete slab. To achieve this, the slab will need a trowelled finish or be surfaced with levelling compound.

● A thin polythene vapour barrier should be laid over the insulation before the boarding is laid; this is essential with mineral-fibre insulation.

● The joints between standard floor-grade chipboards should all be glued, and skirting should be used to pin down the floorboards at the edges.

● A 10 mm expansion gap should exist at the perimeter; the skirting and wall finish will hide it later. This is essential for laminates as well as timber floorboarding, which can expand and contract with the temperature.

without any fixings, but to achieve this the base must be finished to a higher standard.

Most conservatories can be supported on a simple slab of concrete, which is fine if they are built as separated additions over an external door. But if it is designed and built to be integral with your home, or with a view to last as long, you should look towards a more robust foundation that reflects that of the rest of the building. You might choose to use a better base purely for robustness, but there are times when it is essential.

Better bases

Conservatories, given their plastic roofs and glazed walls, are lightweight structures, and being lightweight they shouldn't require a foundation, or at least much of one, should they?

Often not, but it isn't just the weight of a building that can cause it to settle or subside. The ground that it sits on can be quite capable of doing that all by itself, and in some cases the lighter the structure on it, the more damage it can do to it.

A conservatory that sits on a simple slab base, perhaps only 100 mm thick over clay, is likely to be at risk and the first to suffer from the soil's seasonal movement. Because it is formed on the surface and without suitable reinforcement, the concrete can fall and rise with the subsoil beneath it, and if you already have concrete paths that have cracked with this movement over the years, you can assume that the same will happen to your base if you don't take proper measures to improve it.

Reinforced slab bases or raft foundations

Rather than digging deep foundations to avoid the effects of ground movement, you might choose to adopt a slab base that is reinforced with steel mesh or bars. Given the right amount of reinforcement and the right position for it in the slab, it can stiffen the base and allow it to 'float' rigidly over some ground movement without suffering damage. This design, called a raft foundation,

can be the most appropriate form for a conservatory on volatile soil. There are basically two types of raft: the plane type and the edge-beam type; so where should we use them?

We are blessed in the UK with a rich variety of soils: silts, sands, rocks, chalks, gravels and clays – we have them all; the place is a geologist's playground. Some materials, such as chalk, are excellent for building on, and simple slabs beneath conservatories are ideal here. Others,

EQUIVALENT FOUNDATION DEPTHS AND STANDARD SLAB/EDGE-BEAM RAFT BASES NEAR TREES IN SHRINKABLE CLAY SOIL								
Tree species	**Distance from tree to foundation**							
	5 m	8 m	11 m	14 m	17 m	20 m	25 m	30 m
Oak, willow, elm, poplar, eucalyptus, cypress	*3 m*	*2.8 m*	*2.6 m*	*2.4 m*	2.2 m	2 m	1.5 m	1 m
		Edge-beam raft base				Plane raft or simple base		
Ash, chestnut, fir, lime, sycamore, walnut, maple, cedar, yew, spruce, alder, plane, whitebeam	*2 m*	*1.8 m*	*1.5 m*	*1.1 m*	1 m	1 m	1 m	1 m
		Edge-beam raft base				Plane raft or simple base		
Beech, birch, hawthorn, holly, magnolia, pine, fruit trees (apple, cherry, pear, plum, etc.)	1.4 m	1.2 m	1m	1 m	1 m	1 m	1 m	1 m
			Plane raft or simple base					

Note: The depths quoted in the table for conventional foundations could be replaced by raft foundations as an alternative. Figures shown in italic are for edge-beam rafts and those in non-italic for plane rafts or a simple base.

such as sand and clay, may have good load-bearing characteristics but have a tendency to move and cause subsidence. Clay, prevalent in the south and southeast regions, is a shrinkable material that can change in volume dramatically: in the summer it can dry out and shrink, and in the winter it can become waterlogged and heave – either way, it can easily damage an ultra-lightweight addition. A minimum depth of 1 m is usually considered safe in clay soil without trees present, but clay is even more susceptible to change when trees and vegetation exist.

The effects are worst at the surface, which is where bases are formed, but with depth they decrease. Ordinary foundations need to be extremely deep, but they soon become uneconomical to make, and a reinforced raft base may be a more realistic option for a conservatory.

Measure the distance to the tree from the base and read off the minimum depth of excavation for conventional foundations in shrinkable clay soils. If this doesn't appeal to you, a conservatory could be founded on a raft or base shown below the depths (see table opposite).

In the case of hedgerows, it would be appropriate to make a decision based on the worst case species to be found in the hedgerow. Additions that are controlled under the Building Regulations will need to be approved in respect of the foundation design before work starts. All rafts and bases in these situations should be formed over a generous and compacted depth of stone fill.

Tree roots

Cutting through a live root of 50 mm diameter or bigger is not considered to be a good idea. Instead, your base foundation should be designed to bridge over roots, allowing enough space for future growth without the roots' structure exerting pressure on them. Tree roots in turn can exert considerable pressure on ultra-lightweight structures like conservatories, and during growth they may cause structural damage. If you are building close to a tree, seek the advice of a registered arboriculturist.

Removing trees and clay heave

A large, thirsty tree can suck hundreds of litres of water from the ground on a hot day, and if the ground happens to be clay, it will soon become desiccated and shrink dramatically in volume; however, removing a mature tree in the garden could also have a bad effect.

You'll need to consider the age of the tree and its size, because this is a measure of its moisture uptake. In the great carbon cycle of life, trees can't just grow by absorbing the carbon dioxide from the air, they have to add water and minerals to it, and that they get these from the ground. On hot

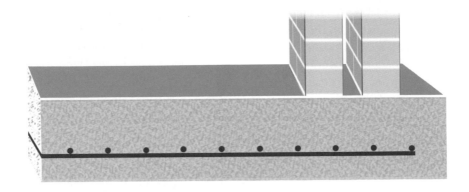

A plane raft foundation showing position of steel reinforcement

sunny days when the process is working hard, trees have to search harder for water, and some species are very good at it: oaks, willows and poplars, to name a few, but also some fashionable garden trees like the Blue Gum eucalyptus. If you have a small one of these in the garden, dig it up now, place it in a large pot and replant it – either that, or make sure you prune it every month.

With a large mature tree removed, the ground can become waterlogged and left to expand in volume. Clay can take up water like a sponge, and this process is known as heave. Beneath a lightweight structure like a conservatory, the resulting heave can lift it up out of the ground and cause

even more damage than shrinkage. There really is only one way to deal with the prospect of clay heave, and that is to use a sacrificial former beneath the raft base of the conservatory. The product is castellated and weak enough to absorb the pressure of heave. Its job is to act as a cushion between your conservatory and the subsoil beneath like the crumple zones on a car. A former can be anything from 50 mm to 300 mm thick, depending on the expected heave

With foundations, it is possible to build in heave precautions at relatively low cost. Lining the walls of foundation trenches with heavy gauge polythene will create a slip plane that can help to prevent heaving clay from exerting pressure on the sides of the foundations.

Plane rafts

The plane raft requires very little structural calculation and normally is made up of a thicker slab, perhaps between 150 mm and 250 mm in depth. It is the less rigid of the two designs, but will still contain two layers of reinforcement positioned, one near to the top and one near to the bottom. These rafts are square-edged bases and are cast over a prepared oversite base of hardcore material, so at least some of the concrete edge can appear above ground level. Depending on your point of view or your design, this can be either be a flaw or a feature.

Edge-beam rafts

This is the type most commonly used in house-building where soft ground is present. In principle it is the same reinforced slab with two layers of reinforcement in the slab, top and bottom, but where it differs is at the edges (beneath the walls). Here, the slab is thicker and a cage of reinforcing bars runs the length of the perimeter.

The slab thickness in the middle is still conventionally between 150 and 250 mm deep, but the edge beam is more likely to be between 450 and 600 mm. The width of the edge beam is always greater than the depth,

normally between 600 and 900 mm. You can assume that, given the average-sized home conservatory, the lower of the quoted figures would be adequate.

A structural engineer's design for an edge-beam raft looks a little more complex, and several different methods of design are accepted. The usual design allows the engineer to spread the weight of the frame and roof carried by the walls through the area of the slab as well. This will be useful if you've got a large, heavier-than-average conservatory with some solid masonry walls and glazed roofing.

Reinforcement for slabs comes in ready-made sheets of steel bars welded into a grid, which can be lapped to cover a larger area or cut to a smaller one. With two grades of steel and several thicknesses of bar, there exists a choice of a dozen grades of mesh fabrics, as they are known, each identified by a code.

Since the number part of the code represents the cross-sectional area of the steel bars per square metre, the higher the number the thicker the bars and the stronger the reinforcement. At the bottom is A98, which is barely more than strong chicken wire and not suitable for anything beyond reinforcing a floor screed or building a henhouse. The next grade up, A142, is the industry standard mesh and is fine for small bases. The table overleaf gives some indication of the base sizes in which they might be used.

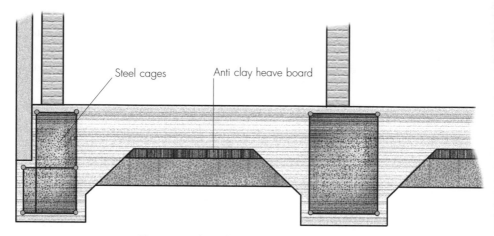

Ground beams reinforced with steel cages formed on site

REINFORCEMENT FOR STRUCTURAL BASES AND PLANE RAFT FOUNDATIONS IN CONSERVATORIES

Grade	Maximum size of base	Thickness of slab	Grade of concrete
MILD STEEL IN SQUARE MESH			
A142	2.5 x 2.5 m	150 mm	C30
A252	3 x 3 m	150 mm	C30
A393	3.5 x 3.5 m	175 mm	C35
HIGH-YIELD STEEL IN RECTANGLE MESH			
B385	4 x 4 m	175 mm	C35
B503	4.5 x 4.5 m	200 mm	C40
B785	5 x 6 m	200 mm	C40

- In plane raft bases two layers of mesh would be used, one 50 mm from the bottom of the slab and one 50 mm from the top.

- In structural bases one layer of mesh would be used.

- Over 30 sq m, a calculated design for a structural base or plane raft should be commissioned by a qualified structural engineer.

Fibre-reinforced concrete

If you can't be bothered with all that heavy steel but still need a reinforced concrete base, there is one other alternative. Fibre reinforcement comes in bags and is sprinkled into the mix while it's being prepared. The fibres are either steel or nylon, and individually are quite small and toothy. The proportion to which they are added to the other ingredients is critical, as it always is with cooking and concreting, but the fibres are designed to be randomly placed in the hardened slab. Together they reinforce it in the absence of steel bars quite effectively, so this method is commonly used for extremely large slabs on industrial developments in place of steel reinforcement.

Steel frame bases

In kit form, box-section steel tubing (aka SHS or square hollow section) is available to form a grid of steel on which the frame can be fixed and flooring can be anchored down. These steel grids sit on a surface of concrete (or at least concrete pads that are strategically placed) via adjustable legs to get it level. The external section is 75 mm square, making it possible to sit a single brick skin on, and the internal tubes, which you might think of as floor joists, are 50 mm square and set apart at standard floor joist centres to allow flooring-grade chipboard or boarding to be span across them. Undoubtedly they speed up construction, but they shouldn't be used without a depth of solid concrete to support them. This concept is more or less the same as that employed with deck construction, although the steel box section is much stronger than timber.

This system best suits the contemporary style of glass walls, but perhaps not a single brick skin dwarf wall. Brickwork leaks unless it is built very thickly, and in cavity wall construction, rain can easily be forced by wind pressure through the mortar joints to the inside – and having to rely on a single skin raised from a metal tube doesn't seem like a good idea.

In the contemporary glass box style, however, without brick walls and with the need for a precise level base for the glass frame to be fixed to, this could be the best method yet, although it should be supported with solid concrete foundations that are suited to your ground conditions.

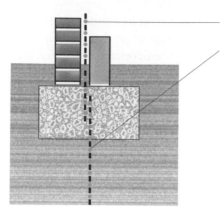

wall centre line

foundation centre line

Determine the foundation centre line and
mark the ground with chalk spray

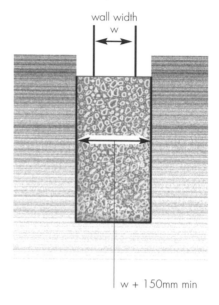

wall width
w

w + 150mm min

Determine the width of the
trench from the wall width

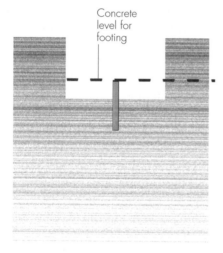

Concrete
level for
footing

Determine the thickness of concrete
(minimum 225 mm) and use pegs or
pins to mark the level required.

Setting out the base

You can't afford to be complacent
about the setting out of the base or
foundations, because getting it wrong
is all too easy. If you happen to get a

conservatory base size wrong it will
also throw out the superstructure, and
for many system-build models the
tolerances for error are not generous.
It does happen from time to time,

however, and extending the base
or digging extra trenches filled with
concrete means extra cost right from
the start. Later on, cutting down
roofing sheets that are also in
standard sizes will result in waste
and more cost. Not only does it
matter to you that your setting out is
correct, it may be critical to the
planning authority, or even Building
Control, that your addition is built to
the correct dimensions and levels.

Boundaries and dimensions

The distance to the boundary can not
only be important from a planning
aspect, given the issues of overlooking
and overshading, but it can also have
an effect under the Building
Regulations with fire spread, and the
Party Wall, Etc. Act. With any non-
combustible (unprotected from fire)
elements on your boundary elevation,
such as windows, plastic or timber
boarding, being limited in area
depending on the distance to the
boundary, some errors in setting out
can be disastrous. On an addition
controlled by Building Regulations,
up to 1 m away from the boundary, a
wall may be allowed with only a small
window. Over 1 m, and the allowance
in these non-combustible areas can be
increased by at least five times, which
can mean the difference between
having your side gable end covered in
PVC-u or the wall having an entrance
door or not. So be sure to double
check your boundary dimensions and

make sure they are correct and
acceptable.

In reality not all of the dimensions
may be critical, but if you have some
discrepancies between the garden
and the plan, now would be the time
to get them resolved and the actual
dimensions approved – before
you form the base. One other
measurement that can be important
is the distance the addition is set
back from the highway, often referred
to as the building line. This is best
described as a notional line that
homes along a street have been
set to or behind but not in front of,
for interests of visual amenity and
highway safety. On corner homes
or front additions, it can be critical.

The physical act of setting out
involves a few wooden pegs or
stakes, some string lines and chalk
spray that can line the ground
clearly when it's time to start
digging. But mostly it involves
measuring and setting corners at
exactly 90°. You can do all of this
with a long tape and some basic
trigonometry – the square root
of the hypotenuse (the diagonal)
should be equal to the sum of the
two opposing sides squared – or
you can hire some professional
setting-out equipment.

Concrete

Bases or rafts are usually formed using
shuttering, plywood sides that are
set up to create a mould into which

concrete can be poured. Formwork has to be robust, since the thought of wet concrete collapsing and pouring out is not a pleasant one. The sides need to be convincingly stake-posted into the ground.

For strip foundations, along with dimensions for the centre line of the trenches and later for the outside of the walls, you will soon need some levels. Once the trenches have been dug, you will need to mark the sides with the level of the concrete proposed – you need some pins on the trench walls or bottom to mark that level and rake the concrete to it. It is entirely possible and quite easy to let the concrete go off without levelling it properly, but your bricklayers will not thank you. With their trade following and the substructure masonry needing perhaps only a few courses of blocks to reach DPC level, it may be impossible for them to level it out over such a short lift. Ordinary concrete is not self-levelling, but it has the consistency of porridge and needs to be raked level.

A product worth considering is a ready-mix concrete with a plasticizer additive that makes it much more fluid and self-levelling, but this isn't widely used. If I've given you the impression that all levels and dimensions are always critical, I apologise; occasionally none of them are. It is simple and best to take some time checking for yourself

or checking with your builder which are, and ensuring that they are correct.

Ready-mix concrete has the advantage of quality control in the mix, guaranteeing its strength and workability. It also takes a lot of the hard work out of the job, particularly when it can be placed directly from the mixer truck into its position on site. You still have some levelling to do, however, because concrete has the consistency of thick porridge and shouldn't actually swim through the trenches to level itself like water.

Raking it to the level required is hard work in itself, but you can make the job easier by knocking in plenty of steel pins to mark the finished level you're after. With bases and rafts, the hard work is in tamping it to the level by using a straight length of timber that will span across the base to the formwork on either side from which your level is taken. Tamping the concrete in this way helps to consolidate it in the same way that vibrating it does, and a gentle sawing and tapping motion combined brings the surface to the level and finish needed. Mixes for ready-mix concrete need to be quoted when you order.

The code ST relates to a standard mix that can be used in most situations where reinforcement isn't required and ground conditions aren't aggressive. Section 4 of BS: 5328: Part 1 defines the materials and proportions for these. GEN code

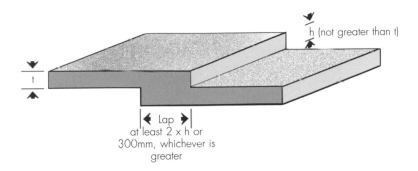

h (not greater than t)

t

Lap
at least 2 x h or
300mm, whichever is
greater

Steps for changes in level should overlap sufficiently (strip foundations).

FOUNDATION MIXES					
Situation	**Standard mix**	**Design mix**	**Strength**	**Slump**	**Compaction**
Simple bases and floor slabs					
Finishings needed	ST 2	GEN 1	10	75	Tamping
No finishings	ST 3	GEN 2	15	75	Beam vibration or trowelled finish
Reinforced bases					
Reinforced rafts, beams, etc.		RC35	35	75	Poker
Trench fill and strip foundations					
Strip foundation	ST2	GEN 1	10	75	Tamping
Trench fill	ST2	GEN 1	10	125	Self-compacting
Sulphate conditions		FND 1-4	35	75	Poker

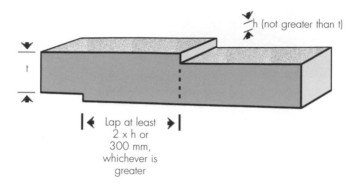

$\frac{h}{2}$ (not greater than t)

t

Lap at least
2 x h or
300 mm,
whichever is
greater

Steps in trench fill foundations

stands for general application as one of several designated mixes, including RC for reinforced concrete situations and FND for foundations in sulphate ground conditions.

Mixing on site

In the small quantities needed for the average conservatory addition, site-mixed concrete is the most economic. A mixer, some cement and all-in ballast (a mixture of sand and aggregates) is all that's needed, and if you have the advantage of being able to mix the concrete close to where it's going to be used, all the better. The other option is ready-mix, which arrives in 5 or 6 cu m loads. Although it's priced per metre, you'll pay a surcharge for any short loads that makes it uneconomical in less than full truckloads.

Suspended or raised floor structures

Reinforced suspended floor slabs

If you do have ground problems or if your floor level is just too high off the ground to permit a slab base or raft, you can adopt the same construction with a suspended concrete floor slab. Here, the dwarf walls will be raised up to the floor level, allowing a reinforcing mesh or fibre-reinforced concrete to strengthen it. A truly suspended slab will bear on the walls and not the ground.

Generally speaking, all suspended floor methods work up to a span of about 5.5 m. If your addition is any wider than this, it is likely that you will need to provide extra load-bearing walls internally to support the floor mid-span. Mesh reinforcing is used instead, as with rafts, but here it is laid near the bottom of the slab only.

SUSPENDED CONCRETE FLOOR SLABS

Span between walls	Mesh size	Concrete grade	Slab thickness
up to 2.4 m	B385	C35	130 mm
2.4–3 m	B503	"	130 mm
3–3.7 m	B785	"	150 mm
3.7–4.3 m	B1131	"	180 mm

TABLE NOTES

- A maximum 63 mm thick cement/sand floor screed finish with domestic floor loads.

- A 40 mm depth of cover between the reinforcement and the underside of the concrete.

- 'B' type mesh has main bars running one way and lesser secondary bars running the other, and is laid in rectangles. It is critically important to place it with the main bars running with the span shown in the tables.

- The mesh should be seated in position on preformed stools to achieve the correct cover to the bottom of the slab.

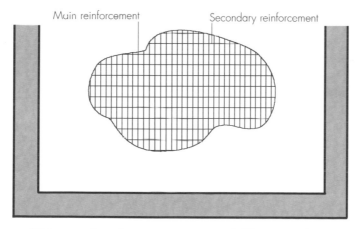

Main reinforcement   Secondary reinforcement

'B' type mesh reinforcement comprises of different size bars.
The largest are the main bars

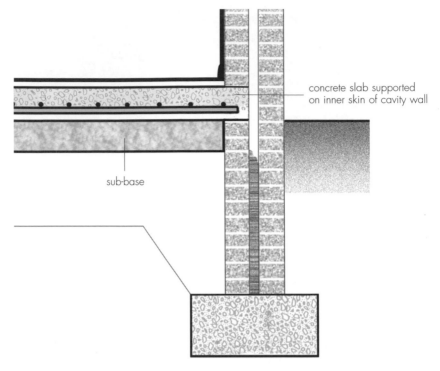

concrete slab supported
on inner skin of cavity wall

sub-base

Suspended floor slabs can be formed with steel mesh
and concrete cast on to the inner leaf for support

Fibre-reinforced concrete can be used as an alternative to steel reinforcing, and should be considered if you're looking for a polished finish to the base. Instead of steel fabric reinforcing mesh to strengthen the concrete, slender plastic or steel fibres are mixed in at the plant or on site to a given proportion, which strengthen it to a similar degree.

Suspended timber floor

Not the best choice for a conservatory, given the high humidity and dramatic temperature changes, timber does, however, make a sound floor structure for a garden room or sun lounge where solid roofing offers a degree of shade and insulation against solar overheating.

If you are using this method for your ground floor, some precautions are needed to avoid rot and decay. The ground beneath it should be covered by a blinding of concrete, around 75 mm thick cast on polythene, to prevent vegetation growth and damp. At least 125 mm of air space should

SUSPENDED TIMBER FLOOR TABLE

Floor joists	C16		Grade	C24	
	400 mm	600 mm	Centres	400 mm	600 mm
50 x 150 mm	3.10 m	2.65 m		3.30 m	2.90 m
75 x 150 mm	3.60 m	3.15 m		3.75 m	3.30 m
50 x 175 mm	3.60 m	3.10 m		3.85 m	3.35 m
75 x 175 mm	4.20 m	3.70 m		4.35 m	3.85 m
50 x 200 mm	4.15 m	3.70 m		4.30 m	3.75 m
75 x 200 mm	4.75 m	4.20 m		4.75 m	4.20 m

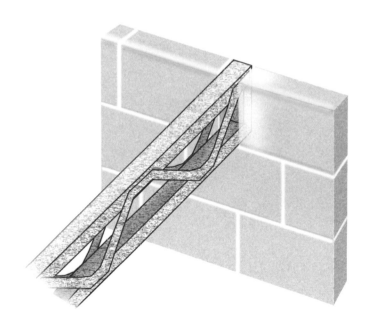

A webbed floor joist will span further than a solid timber joist

exist beneath the floor joists and the ground, and this void should have a good cross-flow from air bricks on both sides, one every 1.5 m of wall. Plastic periscopic air vents are best at achieving this. If you are supporting the joist ends on the inner leaf of the cavity wall, a DPC must be placed beneath them to keep them dry.

Noggins

Timber floor joists need cross-bracing if they aren't to twist, and you can do this either by using offcuts of the joists as solid noggin or herringbone strutting. The latter can be bought in steel strap form or cut on site as 50 x 50 mm softwood. It needs to be positioned in floor spans between 2.5 and 4.5 m in the centre, and for joist spans over 4.5 m as two rows of struts at one-third centres.

Webbed-joist floors

Wooden joists can creak excessively in the high temperature changes of a

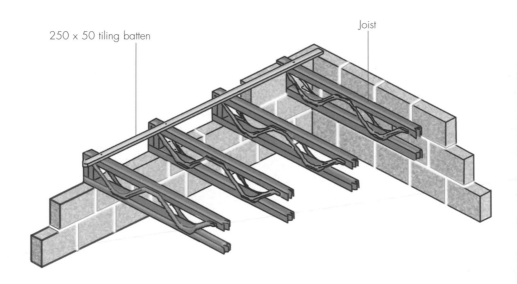

250 x 50 tiling batten

Joist

Webbed floor joists not only span greater distances
but have much less shrinkage than solid timber joists

conservatory when the board fixings are loosened by the shrinkage of the timber. Webbed or truss (TJI) joists don't, because they have a much smaller volume of wood, some with plywood or OSB webs, and others even less with steel braces. They are also lightweight, making them easier to install, and the steel web type can have cable and pipe services running through it without any notching or drilling needed at all, making it perfect for extending services. These joints have the additional advantage of span, which is far greater than ordinary joists, but it is the noise reduction from the absence of a creaking floor that makes them worthwhile. You have to order them to fit from a specialist manufacturer, and some trussed-rafter fabricators have added them to their list of made-to-measure products.

Insulating timber floors

Polyurethane insulation boards can be suspended between joists on battens attached to the sides. A thickness of 100 mm or more will be needed to attain a satisfactory standard, and any pipes or cables have to be run through the void above the insulation boards, so the boards themselves need to be dropped down sufficiently to allow for this. Fixing battens to the joist sides in the strategic position will support the insulation. You can use 200 mm-thick glass fibre to

achieve the same result if you have the depth of joist, but this needs chicken wire fixed beneath the timbers to hold it in place – not always an easy job to do.

Beam and block suspended floors

Precast concrete 'T' beams have the advantage of being able to span greater distances than in situ reinforced slabs or timber joists, and they don't suffer from shrinkage or fungal or insect attack. The infill between beams can be done cheaply with standard wall blocks laid flat and grouted over, or with expanded polystyrene insulation blocks specially made for the purpose. They may be the most expensive option, but you end up with a solid and robust floor you would be happy to lay stone slabs on. The manufacturers normally provide a layout plan to work to showing where the beams are to be positioned, but if you have a hexagonal-ended conservatory, they will expect you to cut the beams to fit the shaped end.

It has become standard practice to sit beams directly on the DPC, and to provide a second DPC on top before proceeding with the dwarf wall structure. This seems to have come about because the placing of the beams has occasionally displaced the first DPC, but if you're careful this shouldn't occur.

Walls and frame

Walls

As can be seen with the contemporary style, it is possible to build a conservatory entirely without walls, but the traditional and most common design approach uses a dwarf wall beneath the windows. which adds some structural strength to the addition and ties in with the existing walls of your home, both physically and aesthetically.

If you're not buying a kit, the height of the dwarf walls is at your discretion, but to determine it, you need to consider how the elevations will work out with the frames and, most importantly, the doors. Windows can be made in any size you require, but it is also possible to buy them in standard sizes off the shelf. This is by far the most economical solution.

Doors, on the other hand, are always a standard height, 2.1 m, over all the frame. The examples shown on page 12 may help you to decide whether you want to include fanlights in your design, and if so, whether you want them above the doors as well as above the windows. With fanlights included over doors the storey height of the elevation is increased, and this has a knock-on effect on the roof pitch and the maximum height of the addition.

Most conservatories are designed from the top down. The position of the sills and first-floor windows above the ground is a fixed distance that can only be changed by lowering the ground level, so this dimension and the roof pitch usually determine the height of the frame.

Dwarf walls must be designed in brick course height and tend to be constructed at between 375 and 750 mm (five and ten courses of bricks). Brick sizes are standard, and with a mortar bed joint included, each course represents about 75 mm.

It's important to include a DPC, which will be positioned beneath the door sill and at least two courses (150 mm) above ground level. Since this represents a step down to ground, you should recognise that most brickwork is measured above DPC level as the point where the superstructure begins. If you'd rather not have a two-course step-down, or if your ground and floor levels are a long way apart, you should look at forming external steps from the doors leading into the garden.

Walls of less than four courses above DPC don't work terribly well - for one thing, the DPC can be thought of as a break in the bond of brick courses. DPCs are usually polythene and the wall can 'slip' on their surface if it isn't held down by enough self-weight; at two or three courses, more weight is required to pin the DPC in place and resist the tendency to slip out of plane. Door frames are normally fixed at the sides and at the head but not at the sill, as to do this would mean puncturing the DPC below. PVC-u windows are screwed down at the cill, usually with 100 mm frame-fixing screws that will really only do their task well when fixed into enough masonry to be secure.

Walls within 1 m of the boundary

Apart from the dwarf walls beneath the windows, there is one other type of wall, which tends to be much underrated. The gable end wall only appears in solid masonry, it seems, if it is close to the boundary of your garden. This goes back to before 1985, when conservatories were controlled under the Building Regulations and within 1 m of the boundary had to have fire-resistant walls to prevent the spread of fire. (In Scotland, this is still the case.) This effectively meant that every rear addition conservatory on semi-detached and terraced homes had at least one side wall that couldn't be framed and glazed.

These boundary line walls are regarded as important when they are controlled under the Building Regulations – a requirement that restricts the external spread of fire from one building to another is not often relaxed, let alone dispensed with.

It might seem odd that this relates to the wall only, and that you could happily comply with a glazed roof pitching onto it and the boundary side. If your brain is taking this a step further than you want it to, walls 'technically' become roofs when they lean at 70° or less (as oppose to being vertical at 90°), but don't go there – sloping walls are strictly for architects.

Fire-resistant glass is available if you are locked into the idea of windows on this side, but it doesn't come cheap. To get 60 minutes of fire insulation from glass (this includes all elements of resistance, including insulation from the radiating heat of a fire) means to have a glazed unit that contains an intumescing core material enclosing the glass layers to a considerable thickness. This isn't double-glazing with an air gap, but a laminated single-glazed product that can chemically react with heat to form a fire barrier. To use this type of glass in the frame of a conservatory would be not only viciously expensive but fairly stupid, since it only works once and the heat from the sun could be enough to activate it on a hot day.

If you are given a relaxation to allow 'non-insulating' fire-resistant glass, 60 minutes fire insulation can be obtained from Georgian-wired polished plate that is much less thick.

Brickwork

The walls of your conservatory may be low, but their quality is just as important as anywhere else. Poor-quality brickwork will always stand out, and will never improve with age.

10 Expert Points

HERE ARE TEN CHECK POINTS TO
ENSURE QUALITY BRICKWORK

1 Mortar should be used within an hour of its mixing. It shouldn't be recycled with extra water once it starts to harden. The best bricklaying sand is never the cheapest, and you'll need to buy the quality sand used by builders, not national DIY superstore brands which are usually very poor.

2 The sand should be kept clean (which means covering it on site or having it delivered in 1-tonne bags) to avoid it becoming a public convenience for the neighbourhood cats.

3 Gauge rods should be used to ensure that the work is vertical and equally coursed.

4 The brickwork must be equal in length and height. Some tolerance is acceptable: up to 5 mm either way in length up to 3 m of wall, and up to 8 mm either way up to 5 m of wall. In height, 3 mm either way is acceptable for dwarf walls up to 1.5 m high; up to 3 m, 5 mm is acceptable. The bricks should rise 300 mm in four courses, with the perps lining up in alternate courses.

5 New brickwork should be protected against bad weather (rain, frost, snow) by hessian sheeting in the winter, and from drying out too quickly beneath a baking sun in the summer.

6 The wall ties should be correctly spaced and embedded into the joints by at least 50 mm.

7 The cavities should be kept clean and free of mortar droppings.

8 The walls should be level and plumb. Up to 10 mm out over any 5 m length of wall may be the industry tolerance for level, but it won't help a conservatory frame. The top course of a dwarf wall needs to be level, when you run a spirit level along it. Plumbness (verticality) can waver a little over 3 m walls, but in dwarf walls up to eight courses high it should be less than 4 mm either way out of plumb. Again, you can check this with a level.

9 Thermal blocks, not bricks, should be used for the split courses of the inner leaf. The blocks are easy to cut by saw, and the use of bricks on the inner leaf (below window cills, for example) destroys the thermal insulation qualities of your wall, producing a cold bridge for heat to transfer through, even if your cavity is insulated. It is essential to cut thermal blocks, even if this takes a little more time.

10 The cavities at the junction with the openings should be closed with a vertical DPC and cut thermal blocks or an insulated cavity closer, a really good invention that takes the workmanship question away. These plastic-foam-filled closers are vertical DPCs and sometimes even frame fixers all in one. The traditional alternative of cutting the blockwork and building in a vertical strip of DPC is thus made redundant, which is not a bad thing, since the task is often badly executed.

Many standardised conservatories are made to brick dimensions, and if you're designing your own, you should look to 215 mm long brick sizes for the length of walls, and 75 mm-high courses. The mortar joints between the bricks should be of equal thickness in every course and of equal width in the perp joints (the vertical ones) if the end result is to look neat. A good bricklayer will take the time to cut bricks to ensure his perp joints are equal, while a lazy one on a price will simply increase the mortar joint width to make up the difference.

For the angled corners of hexagonal-shaped conservatories, special squint bricks can be ordered in advance and look so much better than bricks cut on site. Similarly, bull-nose bricks and other specials can be used beneath the windows or in projecting bands or quoins to make a special feature.

When ordering cement the following figures may prove useful:

40 bags of cement (at 25 kg each) equal 1 tonne (metric)

60 bags of cement (at 25 kg each) equal approximately 1 cu m

Frame
PVC-u frame systems
Any conservatory must be designed to resist the elements, but creating one with some additional robustness will ensure that it stays weatherproof for decades to come. Most are fairly compact in design, and the end panels are easily able to support the side ones against the pressure of the wind, but there is a limit to the span of the panels. If they are too long, the walls and roof may need to be strengthened with a steel or timber portal frame.

If you're buying in your conservatory as a design and erect package, the supplier will take care of this design and should be able to provide structural calculations to justify it. The manufacturer should provide you with a structural guarantee for the superstructure in these cases. If, on the other hand, you are self-designing the conservatory, an engineer's involvement should also be sought. The frame manufacturers should tell you what the limits are for their product – but as a rule of thumb, when conservatories exceed 6 m in length, you should at least check the limits.

Large conservatories and lateral stability.
The weight of your addition will help to keep the conservatory in place, but horizontal pressures are brought to bear as well, and they don't help at all. Horizontal loads aren't so easy to take care of. They come from one of two sources: the wind or, in the case of basement and retaining walls, the ground.

Wind loading can vary tremendously, and some method

of calculating the maximum wind pressure on a wall has had to be derived by British Standards over the years. BS:6399 does this and allows the design engineer to pick basic wind speeds off the map appropriate for your region and then tweak them with a series of factors based on your home's altitude and level of exposure or shelter. The basic wind speed itself can vary from 36–48 m/sec regionally, so the resulting pressure can be very different from one garden to another. From this, the pressure or load on 1 sq m of wall can be derived and its stability assessed. Whether it will stand up depends on the strength of the frame and masonry used, and the size of the panel between buttressing ends.

This level of analysis in entirely unnecessary for standard-sized conservatories, but for anything on the large size it becomes an issue, not just for the frame but the brick walls as well, if they are high. For standard cavity wall, large would be over 8 m long, but a dwarf wall would be able to resist wind load over a greater length. Your buttressing frame and wall is the one running at 90° to the dwarf wall, and its job is to complete the box and prop it up against the wind.

PVC-u frames have a little metal tubing inside them for strength, but this isn't enough and wind posts may have to be added between the frames on larger models. These posts are hollow-sectioned steel posts that can be built in to the wall and tied top and bottom to transfer the load into other structural elements, such as the eaves beam or a cross tie. You can buy proprietary ones made of stainless steel, or you can get a steel fabricator to form one to suit your needs; often, plastic-coated 75 x 75 mm SHS steel posts are used as part of a structural frame for large conservatories that would suffer structural damage otherwise. In England and Wales, large conservatories have always been described as being over 30 sq m in floor area, and approval under the Building Regulations has been necessary for these since 1985.

Apart from the thermal standards applied by these regulations, the other difficulty comes with the structure and the issues of lateral stability. If you're buying a designed and manufactured package, the structural design calculations and details should come with it for this purpose. If you're preparing your own design to be constructed, you'll need the services of a structural engineer to calculate the loads applied and resolve the size of beams and ties for the frames. They may still be able to use frame analysis methods that will allow you to have 'standard' frames prefabricated in steel hollow sections or timber off-site. This will be a tremendous help to your builders and speed up the construction process on site.

System-build assembly

Plastic conservatories have one major advantage over timber: they've seen investment in a system-build approach to make them quick to install on site. Some frame manufacturers have embarked on a bit of product evolution and invented new ways of fitting the parts together more simply and quickly, the aim being to pre-assemble much of the frame in the factory. A typical roof might arrive in 15 component packs for a standard-sized conservatory plus the glazing, but six packs plus glazing can often be achieved with system-build kits. Assembly steps that can only be taken on site are done with 'snap lock' or 'click fit' joints, which don't need bolts, screws or silicone mastic, the prime elements of the erection process.

Speed of build might not be an issue if you're not a housing developer, but system-build kits have a market with home owners embarking on DIY, too. They make the process much simpler, and some even provide the bits in colour-coded boxes to match a box-opening sequence. PVC cappings and finishings that cover aluminium pieces are neatly paired with them, and the instructions seem to be practically idiot-proof – on one that I've seen, the step-by-step directions were boldly printed with one step per page. OK, so you're not going to be able to put a frame together in the same time it takes experienced fitters to. But this system leaves much less room for error, and it is safe to say that the kits are much better designed, made and packaged than any flat-pack furniture you've ever bought – I'd be happy enough to discover that all the parts were there and the drawer bottoms weren't made of hardboard.

The systems mean that an average 3 x 3 m model can have its roof framed and glazed in one and a half hours on site, about half the time it takes using the bolt and silicone joint types.

With some innovative components being patented by the designers, not all the systems are identical, and you need to shop around to find the easiest for DIY assembly. Some have spirit levels built into the ridge member, which means you can be certain the piece goes in level.

Most systems include some dual-purpose elements like a fascia board that also supports the glazing and thus does away with an eaves beam; or an eaves beam that doubles as a fascia, and so on.

Given the incompatibility between polycarbonate sheets of roofing and the soft metal of lead flashings, plastic flashings are also available. The ridge pieces are designed and made to lock in with stepped flashing pieces extruded from PVC, looking rather like preformed stepped cavity trays, that can weather the abutment between wall and roof.

10 Expert Points

A TYPICAL PROCEDURE FOR A PVC-U HIP-END FRAME IN 10 STAGES

1 The sill of the frame is positioned on top of the dwarf wall once a DPC has been fully bedded to the masonry. It's important that the floor damp-proof membrane (DPM), which is often polythene sheeting, is turned up the wall and overlaps the wall DPC to form a continuous barrier against damp.

2 All fixed glass is then removed from the frames before they are fixed. Beginning at the centre frame, each in turn is fixed down, with a seal of silicone mastic being used beneath the sill. The method of fixing down the frames is dependent on their position in relation to the base and the DPC. If the frames are to be fixed directly to the base, frame fixing plates are ideal; screwed to the underside of the sill, they can be fastened mechanically to the concrete of the floor slab. Since they are made of thin stainless steel, they are comfortably bedded beneath floor finishings such as screed or tiling. These frame fixings are also ideal where the DPC is directly under the sill – driving a screw type fixing through the sill and the DPC to anchor it down to the wall is less than ideal, as the DPC is there to provide a continuous barrier against rising damp, and puncturing it with screw holes every 600 mm isn't going to help. In this situation the frame ties protrude internally. They can bend down the inner face of the brick wall to be secured within the cavity with plugs and screws or built in to the inner skin. As mentioned elsewhere, it isn't a good idea to have a single brick skin dwarf wall, which will be less than rain-resistant, but if you do, the ties could be bent down and fixed against it internally before the wall is finished, either with dry-lining or plaster render.

3 The window frames are joined together via coupling mullions or corner posts, and are secured in place by screws at no more than 400 mm centres but within 150 mm of the corners at the top and bottom. The frames that directly abut masonry existing walls of your home are fixed with expanding bolts or similar types of mechanical fixings.

4 The eaves beam that runs along the top of those frames to support the roof is then fixed in position and the joints at the corners are spliced together, using aluminium cleats that are screwed over them for strength.

5 The ridge beam is positioned and held in place with the glazing bars and hip bars that will support the glazing. Proprietary quick-locking systems are used to form these joints – for example, the eaves and ridge beams often have captive bolts pre-fixed within the extrusion for quick assembly on site. For hipped roofs, the hip beams are gathered at the ridge and clamped to the end, often in the form of a die-cast piece.

6 The first set of glazing bars, those that run alongside the existing wall, are fixed directly to it through their sides with plugs and screws or expansion bolts.

7 A remedial DPC tray is installed in the masonry wall (if it is cavity wall construction and faced brickwork) along the line of the abutment above the first glazing bars. The lead flashing that will cover the abutment can also be installed at this time before the glazing is done and while access is easier. Some stepped cavity trays incorporate a lead flashing pre-bonded

WALLS AND FRAME

in pieces to the DPC tray for quicker installation; the lead has to be folded up until the first glazing sheets are installed and then it can be dressed down.

8 The roof can then be glazed, with each individual panel being located into the ridge panel between the PVC-u rain baffle and the sealing gasket, which is normally a TPE extruded material. The bars are covered by PVC-u caps, which also have sealing gaskets of the same material and are snap-locked in place to seal against rain penetration.

9 A polyurethane foam bung is located at the joint between the hip bars and the ridge piece, and is sealed in place with silicone mastic before the inner finishing piece is fitted internally.

10 The procedure is completed by fitting trims such as ridge cresting and finial pieces, window boards and glass in windows and doors. Guttering and downpipes are added on completion, together with any surface water drains required to dispose of the rainwater.

Snagging

When the job is finished you can check it over and create a list of defects that need attention. In the industry this is standard practice and is known as snagging – a more onomatopoeic word you could not have found. The question list overleaf should help you with your snagging.

Cavity wall ties

For a very long time cavity walls were built with 50 mm cavities, until the 1980s, when we began to fill them with insulation. In 2002, when external wall insulation standards were increased to a maximum U value of 0.35 w/m sq k, wider cavities became standard to allow for a greater thickness of insulation, 65 or 75 mm wide, depending on the type of inner leaf and insulation. With these you can still use the standard wall ties at maximum 900 mm horizontal and 450 mm vertical spacings. If you want an even wider cavity, you should use a suitable tie, such as the vertical twist type, to maintain the structural bond, even for a low wall; for this, the maximum horizontal centres are reduced to 750 mm from the standard 900 mm.

Cavity wall insulation

Don't be tempted to miss out on the insulation of your cavity walls – the cost is negligible, and it will help, in conjunction with an insulated ground floor, to reduce the heat loss from any

117

SNAGGING

APPEARANCE

- Are the windows and doors fitted square, upright and plumb, and is the ridge level? Use a spirit level to check.

- Are the exposed parts undamaged? The protective plastic film that comes stuck to PVC-u products should only be removed once all the work is finished.

- Are there any cracks in the welds of the windows? The welds are the mitres at the corners of frames, formed in the factory – but not always perfectly.

- Are all the internal and external trims fitted correctly?

- Has all debris been removed, and has the area been left clean?

- Do the window and door heads align on a level eaves?

GLASS

- Is the glass fitted in accordance with the specification and with Building Regulations for safety in critical locations?

- Are the sealed units intact and neither cracked or leaking? If the glass mists up on the inside of the cavity, the seals have failed.

- Are any low-e glass units fitted the right way around?

SEALS

- Are all the silicone mastic joints sealed smoothly, continuous and correctly shaped?

- Are the surrounding walls and frames free from excess sealant? Using mastic sealant correctly is a skilled and practiced job, and a messy finish reveals a shortcoming in both these qualities.

WEATHERING

- Are the roof panels sealed at the perimeter edges with flashings, and are the glazing caps locked tightly over the bars?

- Is the flashing to the wall wide enough and lapped at any joints? Lead should be dressed 150 mm over both surfaces and of Code 4 grade.

- Has a remedial cavity tray DPC been fitted over the flashing to the wall? This should be lapped if jointed, and have drainage perp ends. Trays are only fitted to cavity walls.

- Have the gutters been fixed correctly and to adequate falls? Are they connected to the surface water drainage system or a soakaway at least 5 m away?

- Are all drainage channels correctly positioned on the outer face of sills? Door frames can't be reversed to open the other way if the drainage channels will then drain internally. These channels are positioned to let rainwater run out rather than in, so they can be fitted the wrong way around.

THE NUMBER OF WALL TIES NEEDED

| Cavity width | MAXIMUM SPACINGS | | Number of ties per 1 sq m of wall |
	Vertical	Horizontal	
50–75 mm	900 mm	450 mm	2.5
75–100 mm	750 mm	450 mm	3.0
100–150 mm	450 mm	450 mm	4.9

conservatory. With dwarf walls, you can expect to see the inner leaf of blocks or bricks built first and the insulation attached to it before the external skin of facings goes up. Cavity wall insulation is installed in this way and is never pushed down into the cavity afterwards, even if the wall is low. I have known of unscrupulous builders using strips of insulation in the cavity only at the top of the wall for appearance.

Matching bricks

Consider yourself lucky if you can find the same brick that your existing home was built with and it still looks the same. Bricks, like cakes, never come out of the oven looking identical, and there is some variation from batch to batch, let alone from year to year or decade to decade – all of which presents any addition to the home with a problem: do you plough all your efforts into looking for the nearest match, or do you go for a contrast?

The nearest match idea works up to a point. To my way of thinking the colour should come first when trying to match bricks, but plenty of builders disagree, suggesting that the colour will change as the brick weathers in and blends with the existing bricks. Well, maybe, given 20 years of traffic pollution an orange brick will darken slightly, but will it ever become a dark red? – I think not, at least not in our lifetimes. It's worse with yellow stock bricks that turn black after a century of grime: do you match to the original colour – in the hopes that one day it will start to look as bad – or do you find a colour that blends today?

After colour should come texture – not the other way around. A brick that has the same colour but a different facing surface won't be so noticeable as one with the same texture but a different colour. Give yourself a

119

chance and obtain several options in brick sample packs from your supplier. One brick is not enough; three or four are needed to see the potential for variation. Mix them and stand them up against the original and look at them in the half-light, in the sunlight and in the shade, and only then decide.

If you can't find a brick that looks anything better than a bit different, it might be best to adopt a contrast and look for bricks that are obviously different. In this way, the contrast can be viewed as an architectural statement and not a failed case of matching in. For a contrast, you need colours that are in the same tone, and a colour wheel will help just as much here as it does in choosing paint and furnishings. A sandy, buff-coloured brick will not match so well with a red or orange facing as it will with a brown colour. Harmonious colours or those from the same tonal range work best together, and if you are only building a few courses high, a deliberate contrast is often the most appropriate choice anyway.

Solid walls

When you consider it, a solid wall facing a boundary is not an undesirable thing and offers some privacy to both neighbours. It also gives some extra stability to the construction, as well as some valued sound and thermal insulation. If you are going to invite some plants into your conservatory to share it with you, a masonry wall will also store much of the day's heat and release it gradually at night, as well as affording you the exciting opportunity of growing some exotic climbers (see page 165).

Every gardener knows that on a summer's day a south-facing brick or stone wall acts as a heat bank, but one behind glass will do an even better job throughout the year. In the Eden Project, the natural earth bank does the same and indeed the Biomes were positioned to take full advantage of this effect. A solid gable wall, boundary or no boundary, is not a bad thing at all.

Stone walls

Brickwork isn't the only form of masonry: stone walls look terrific inside and out. If your home has been built with stone, it is likely to be indigenous to the area, and it's important to source it locally to match in. Stonework does vary from region to region, not just in the type of stone but also in the way it is laid.

If stone has a drawback at all, it is that the conservatory framework of windows around the perimeter means that the dwarf wall must be pretty much perfectly level at its head. Even when it is shaped and coursed, stone is hard to lay that level, so a thick mortar bed may have to be provided for the frames to be set on, and the projecting cills may need to hide it.

Don't be tempted to lay a dry stone face without the cavity behind it being designed to drain away large quantities of wind-driven rain – and stone isn't always frost-resistant. Mortar spacing dabs aren't really any better, as the mortar can transmit salts through to the surface to create efflorescence. This happens a lot with brickwork these days, but it does wash off and give up in time. Stones are best when they are bedded down flat on their natural quarry bed, and the quarry supplying it can mark this for you.

Where flint walls are to be formed, concrete blocks of standard and regular size that have flints set in the face are available. The stones project from the concrete surface so that when the block wall is built they can be pointed in carefully to lose the 'block joints'. Using these blocks, you have both the level surface that you need for the frames and the rustic appearance of traditional flint walling. Even if your home doesn't already possess flintwork, it can add a pleasing contrast to the brick walls of a country house.

Fielded or moulded panels

A cheaper alternative to building a dwarf wall uses panels as part of the framework. These are effectively solid windows, if that makes sense. Moulded PVC-u panels are extruded

Solid moulded panels (left) are likely to outlive thinner fielded panels (right)

with polyurethane core the same as external doors in this material. They have good thermal insulation properties and allow the construction work to proceed much more quickly in the absence of any bricklaying or plastering. They can be easily washed down, will never rot or need decorating but will always look like plastic panels, at least in white. Mahogany- or teak-finished PVC-u has a distinct advantage in this situation, as in panels it can look like real hardwood – well, from a distance in poor light.

In traditional timber construction panels, instead of being moulded, are fielded using either solid timber frames or plywood that is decorated with mouldings glued and pinned in place. I've seen ply used for this just before it's been torn off and replaced with something sensible. The lower walls of any building are prone to rain splashing, accidental damage and general wear and tear, and this is not the place to skimp on durable construction – even 12 mm exterior-grade ply can warp and split quite happily. Some better-quality timber framed conservatory manufacturers have switched to routing fielded panels out of 44 mm solid wood – the very material thickness used in the styles and rails of external doors. When the wood has been vacuum-treated with preservative, it can be guaranteed for at least 15 years.

At the cheaper end of the market, softwood pine can be used and treated with stain to achieve a natural finish; at the top end you get hardwoods such as iroko. Whichever you choose, remember that timber of any kind in contact with the ground will be susceptible to damp and rot. The base plinth must include a DPM that is dressed over a DPC beneath the panels and their sole plates. Plastic is a DPC by itself, of course, but since damp can penetrate the gaps between panels if they aren't totally sealed, it pays to use a DPC beneath them and to silicone-mastic the joints.

Steel-framed dwarf wall kits are also available, very much the kind of construction popular in the United States, with lightweight galvanised steel channels bolted down to a steel tube base and clad over. They don't rot, and they are totally vermin-proof because the panels are covered by ultra-thin steel-profiled sheets as well. The worst thing about them is they are designed to be faced up by a false brick veneer, much like the stone cladding we used to glue to our homes in the 1970s. If you do use this panel system, you might want to show your home a bit more respect and replace it with render over expanded metal lathing instead.

Glass block panels and walls

Glass blocks aren't new but they are back in fashion, notably in contemporary design and usually as internal screens, but they can also be

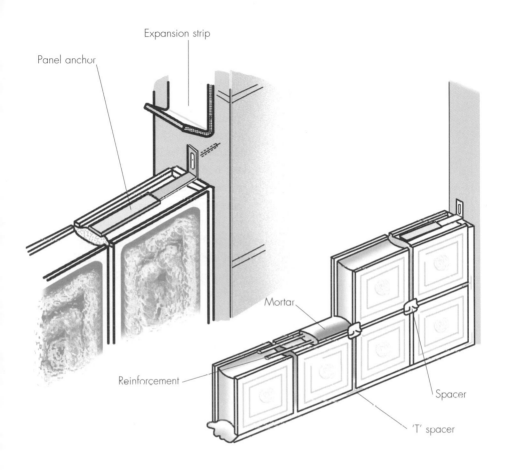

Conventional glass block laying in mortar adhesive

used as panels for the external walls of a conservatory or sun lounge. They can be installed dry within a framework, and dedicated lightweight systems are available to this end, comprising an outer frame that can be fixed to the surrounding structure and both horizontal rails supporting the blocks and vertical dividers. You can use glass block walls inside – as

dividing walls that let the light through but also provide excellent sound insulation from one part of your addition to another and in this respect they make ideal in-fillings to enlarged openings surrounding a door between the house and the conservatory – or outside. If you choose to use them for part of an external wall, it is important to drill

123

A glass block wall

to create a more obscured finish and cut about 80 per cent of light transmission.

Laying them couldn't be easier. Armed with a small trowel for spreading the adhesive mortar, a level and a sponge for wiping them clean, anyone can build with glass blocks. All you need to check is that you are putting in the spacers and the work is level plumb and true as you go. Let the mortar set for an hour before you try to strike it off from where it has squeezed out of the joints and don't let it dry out totally before you sponge any surplus off the face of the blocks themselves. The manufacturers also provide reinforcing bars which can be simply pressed down into the bed of adhesive before the next

out a series of 12 mm holes along the horizontal rails and the sill for drainage. Without it, they will act as collection channels for rainwater running off the glass fence. If your framework is in timber, it goes without saying that it should be treated with preservative.

Not only has the range of colours and finishes expanded with their popularity, but also the sizes of blocks. From 115 x 115 mm, up to the standard size of 190 x 190 mm and on up to the large 298 x 298 mm. The latter weigh over 7 kg each, compared to the standard ones at 2.4 kg. There are even ventilator blocks and end blocks, glass tile ends, corner and curved radius blocks on the list of extras because you can't cut or drill glass blocks. In truth, about all you can do to alter them is sandblast them

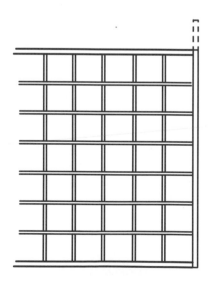

A Framelight system

course of blocks are laid and these are essential for panels over a certain length (around 1400 mm) but highly recommended anyway.

If your panels are relatively small, you might prefer to build them first and install them to the frame opening later. Some of the dry-fix systems are designed for this but do remember that you are going to have to lift the finished panel into position and it is going to be heavy. The framing can consist of planed timber that slots into plastic sleeving for a clean and neat finish. Stainless steel anchor brackets and the use of silicon mastic for sealing around the perimeter and caulking the joints between blocks create a weatherproof panel.

There are two uses that make glass blocks exceptionally superior to glass panes. The first being that you can build a curved panel out of them very effectively. Of course there is a minimum radius for the standard-size blocks to achieve this but it is only about 1650 mm and it would be easily achieved. The second is on boundary walls where fire-resistance is required. A special glass block that has been tested and certificated for this purpose is needed here, but they are commonly available as the only difference between them and the standard ones is a thicker wall of glass. Instead of the usual 8 mm, the walls of these are increased to 26 mm, making the overall block width 100 mm instead of 80 mm.

ADVANTAGES OF GLASS BLOCKS

- They are strong and burglar resistant

- They have good sound and thermal insulation values (with 8 mm-thick walls and a 62 mm-wide centre, they have a thermal transmission U value of 2.9 W/m.sq.deg.k – slightly below standard double-glazing with a low e-coating).

- Easy to build with

- Available in a good range of colours and finishes.

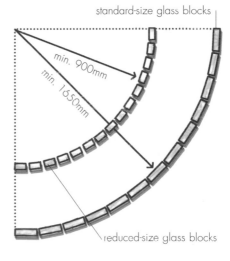

A curved glass block panel

CHAPTER SEVEN

Roof

Onwards and upwards

One of the drawbacks of any addition to the home, be it conservatory, sun lounge or whatever, is the further you go out in depth the lower the roof pitch must become. That's trigonometry for you – not content with making your school days miserable, it gets in the way of extending the house. With roof tiles, roof pitch is critical, and every manufactured tile has a minimum pitch to which it can be laid and still relied upon to keep the rain out.

Glazed roofs, however, are not so demanding, and low pitches are common on conservatories; given the position of the upstairs windows and the depth of the addition, pitched roofs are often no more than 20° and sometimes even less. Technically speaking, even flat roofs have a pitch to them because a slope angle of less than 10° is described as flat. If the rainwater is going to run off efficiently to the gutters, a good fall is essential and it pays to keep the pitch as steep as you can.

Many conservatory lean-to roofs are technically flat roofs because of this, and there are roofing systems glazed with polycarbonate that have received BBA (British Board of Agrement) approval down to 2.5°: at this slope the water will trickle off to the gutter, where the fall is about the same around the fascia. I don't doubt that

it's a testimony to the improvements in plastic roof technology that this can be done, with sealing between the glazing bars and the flashings of the system roof, but I wouldn't pitch a roof made of anything at that angle – while it may work perfectly well when new, it is going to age. With age can come greening from algae and lichen, which coats a polycarbonate roof just as easily as a glass or tiled one, with age can come distortion from ground movement and solar heating, and with age can come deflection from wind and snow loads. Buildings don't stay new for long, and that is why it is wise to build in some robustness. A low pitch will advance the ageing process and, with it, all the bad things that can happen to a roof later in life.

The steeper the angle, the faster rainwater runs off and the greater the self-cleaning ability of the glazing, reducing the susceptibility to algae growth and leakage. As if that isn't enough for you, roof pitches of between 30° and 45° degrees look better on most homes, since they reflect the main roof angle.

Holding down the roof

Odd as it may seem, solid roofs are not always as well anchored down as glazed ones. A solid roof covered by slates or lightweight tiles can be lifted by the suction of the wind passing over it. To compensate, steel straps are fixed over the wall plate and down the walls. Roofing systems that use polycarbonate sheets have to combat this wind suction differently: here, the sheets are locked down by the glazing bars and their covers, and these bars are screwed down to the rafters and eaves beams. Screws are normally installed at a maximum of 400 mm and should be large enough for the task at hand – the primary object here is to try to hold down the roof to stop it blowing away, not to support it. The potential wind uplift force can exceed the weight of the roof by many times.

With holding-down straps that usually have to be fixed to the masonry of the inner leaf, the fixing isn't always easy. Lightweight aerated blocks can't be nailed into with any conviction, and plugging and screwing these straps on is essential if they are to work. The dead weight of the roof is sometimes enough to hold itself down against wind uplift, but for the cost it is worth putting straps on anyway, particularly if you have a wide overhanging soffit that the wind can push against.

Plastic roofing
Clear acrylic sheeting
Acrylic has better light-transmission properties than polycarbonate, which is a posh way of saying it's clearer, but it seems to be restricted in the construction industry to shower doors or the windows of public aquariums, the latter demonstrating just how strong and yet flexible the material can be. Transparent tunnels that let you walk through the underwater environments, such as the 112 m-long one at Deep Sea World in Fife, are made of acrylic and are strong enough to resist the kind of pressure that 4,500,000 l of water can exert, while we safely walk beneath it. Granted, the walls are considerably thicker than you'd want for a conservatory roof, but acrylic sheeting is a versatile material.

In most DIY or hardware stores acrylic sheeting is sold for use in greenhouses or secondary double-glazing, which is a shame, because it has greater potential than that. Like polycarbonate, it lacks security and shouldn't be used where open-plan layouts are proposed without a secure

ACRYLIC SHEETING		
Type	Weight	Light transmission
U value		
6 mm thick clear	7.14 kg/sq m	95%

internal door to your home being present.

If this makes it sound completely unsuitable for roof work, some leading skylight manufacturers have been using it in preference to glass in their products for many years. It makes for a good lightweight skylight dome on a flat roof, but although it doesn't break, it is a 'soft material' that is scratched easily, so it can't be cleaned with anything abrasive, which will scour the surface with fine scratches.

Acrylic has the distinct advantage over glass of being workable on site and easily sawn, cut and drilled. 8 mm is a minimum thickness for use in roofing, but rafters need to be at a maximum of 400 mm centres, even for this thickness, and it still won't feel good for anybody wanting to get on it for maintenance or repair.

Polycarbonate sheeting

Most conservatory roofs are glazed with polycarbonate sheets. In 20 mm thickness with a cellular structure made up of five walls, this kind of roof sheet has considerable resistance against breakage. In truth it is pretty much unbreakable under impact: manufacturers claim it is 200 times stronger than glass. However, all this is irrelevant because polycarbonate roofing doesn't tend to fail in this way. Although it has a multi-walled cellular structure, the cavities inside the 20 mm sheets are open-ended and the sheets are cut to fit the roof shape, with the ends taped up on

Polycarbonate roof sheets in standard widths supported by a system of glazing bars

CLEAR ACRYLIC ROOFING

Advantages	Disadvantages
Cheap	Poor thermal insulation
Stronger than glass	Poor airborne sound insulation
Lightweight and resistant to cracking	Expands in hot weather
Excellent light transmission	Poor security
	Difficult to weather with lead flashings
	Difficult to obtain in suitable size and thickness

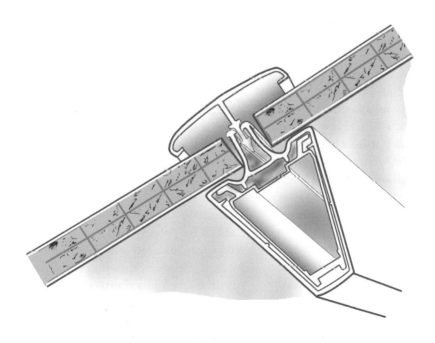

Twin wall polycarbonate sheeting secured by glazing bar and capping installation. In other words, the cavities aren't hermetically sealed in their manufacture, the way double-glazed windows are sealed, which means they offer less resistance to the passage of heat.

It is difficult to find accurate U values quoted by the manufacturers because of all this, but it is still perhaps the most relevant question to ask. Conservatory companies are keen to point out the U values of windows and doors because they are impressive, but are often less talkative on the subject of polycarbonate roofing. It's a shame we haven't found a better option, because I can't help but think that the cost of double-glazed windows and insulated cavity dwarf walls is rather wasted if all the heat goes out through the roof. Heat, as we all know, rises, and all the insulation in the sides simply means that a higher percentage of it will rise out through the roof instead if it isn't better insulated. This is where the problems of open-through conservatories lie, and in effect a poorly insulated roof to any home addition is a Thermos flask without a cap.

Compared to single glazing, the twin walls of polycarbonate sheets are much better insulated, but compared to the low-e coated or argon-filled double-glazing we use today, polycarbonate is hopelessly flawed. Another reason why you might not want to open up your home beneath

a plastic roof is security. Adding doors with multi-locking points and windows with 60 mm thick steel reinforced frames and locking window handles is great, but a polycarbonate roof can be sawed through with any type of serrated edge – even a junior hacksaw will even cut it, ideal for burglars in a hurry.

The good points of polycarbonate are that is cheaper than glass, quick to install and lightweight. Because it is affordable, more people can enjoy the ownership of a conservatory, and by being lightweight it doesn't impose a dead load on the walls, which means they can comprise continuous window frames around the perimeter. The light weight has, however, led cowboy builders to not bother supporting it against the house wall and to use self-adhesive (sticky-back) tape to weather this abutment instead of lead. To be fair to lead, it is a metal, albeit a soft one, and is traditionally used as a weathering against hard materials, where it can be hammered with a rubber mallet to a snug fit – not something easily achieved between a bouncy plastic roof and a brick wall.

Because polycarbonate sheeting is frequently installed at a very shallow pitch, it can mean that water is slow to run off, and in a north-facing aspect or close to trees, algae will render it permanently green. I've known people in this situation give up the bi-annual chore of scrubbing it clean and succumb to living beneath a

POLYCARBONATE ROOFING SPECIFICATION

Type	Weight	tight Transmission	U value minimum*
10 mm thick twinwall (clear)	1.7 kg/sq m	79%	3.0
16 mm thick triplewall (clear)	2.7 kg/sq m	76%	2.3
(opal)	"	48%	"
(bronze)	"	35%	"
25 mm thick multiwall (clear)	3.5 kg/sq m	55%	1. 8
(opal)	"	20%	"
(bronze)	"	20%	"

* U-values shown are minimums and may be higher in practice, particularly where ends and joints aren't fully sealed. The higher the U value, the more heat passes through and hence the worse the insulation. The lower the number, the better the insulation. In 2004 loft insulation standards in new homes permit U values no higher than 0.16; even the best glazing lets heat escape through it ten times faster than this.

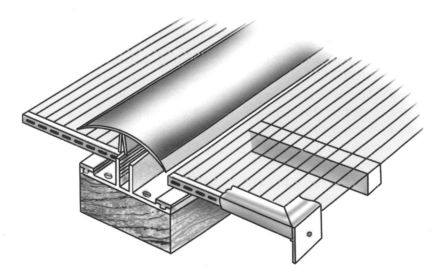

Polycarbonate sheets with glazing bars supported by timber rafters

131

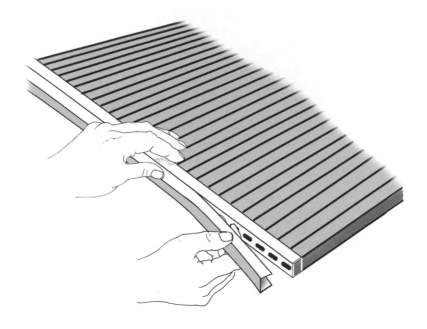

End capping of multi-wall polycarbonate to seal the cavities

pond-coloured roof. You can't blame them: the polycarbonate itself may not break under your weight if you get up on it to keep it clean, but the sheets are all too often delicately supported on thin glazing bars and formed into a structure that simply isn't designed to carry your weight. No offence intended.

You can see from the table on page 131 that not until a 25 mm multi-wall thickness of this material is used, do the thermal insulation U values become comparable with double-glazing. Unfortunately, when you get to this thickness with its extra walls, the amount of light that passes through it is dramatically reduced. Barely more than half passes through, and a 'clear' polycarbonate roof can be referred to as translucent rather than transparent. In shaded form, this fraction reduces dramatically to 20 per cent.

Pretty much all polycarbonate sheets sold as roofing have a Class 1 (BS:476:Pt 7) fire spread rating, making them suitable for use anywhere in dwellings.

Typical DIY polycarbonate roof
Because polycarbonate is so easily available in sheet form, you can obtain it and create a simple lean-to roof with it yourself.

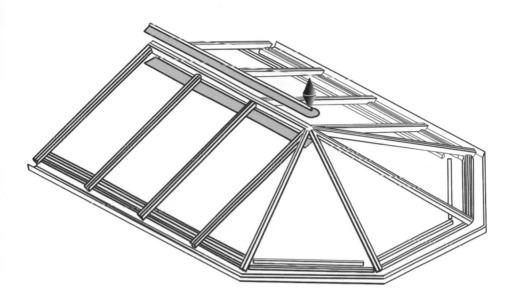

Roof system of glazing bars, eaves bars and ridge

POLYCARBONATE ROOFS

Advantages	Disadvantages
Cheaper	Noisy during rainfall/can be holed by hailstones
Obscured for built-in shading	Poor airborne sound insulation
Lightweight and resistant to cracking	Expands in hot weather
Thermally better than single glass	Creaking and can buckle under extreme heat
Commonly available	Poor light transmission in its insulating multi-wall form
	Awkward to weatherproof with lead flashings

133

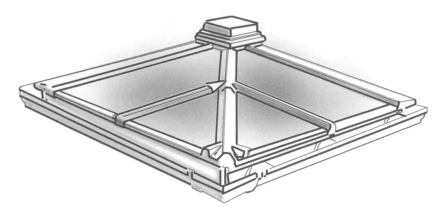

Ridge and eaves capping to finish

Cutting and preparing the sheets

Calculate the sheet sizes and number of glazing bars needed before you start, and prepare the sheets, cutting them to size.

You can cut this material parallel along the flutes or (voids) with a sharp knife, but otherwise a fine-tooth saw is needed. If you do have to cut around curves, you'll need a suitable jigsaw, but generally speaking, cutting this material is easy. As with many plastics, a static electric charge builds up during cutting, and sawdust is prone to sticking to it and can get in the voids. If you leave it to stand for a while, the charge will dissipate and you can vacuum the sheets.

Unlike double-glazing, the hollow pockets aren't hermetically sealed, but you do have to tape the ends up to try and limit the build-up of condensation in them. The top end gets sealed with a weatherproof tape

and the bottom with a perforated breathable tape that allows trapped vapour to be released.

You can save yourself a lot of trouble and waste by designing your conservatory to suit standard sheet sizes. Look for product information on sizes before you finalise a design.

Cavity trays to facing brick walls

Before the sheets go up and block the access, you need to prepare the flashing and install a cavity wall tray DPC at the abutment between the roof and wall. Trays aren't necessary on external walls that are clad with rendering, boarding or tile hanging; if these are in good condition, they should keep out the rain. Because facing brickwork in cavity walls is only 112 mm wide (single brick), it is porous and prone to being penetrated by wind-driven rain. It didn't matter when it was the external skin of a cavity wall, but now that its part of the brick skin becomes internal to your conservatory, it's a problem. You can't afford to let rainwater saturate the wall above the roof and drain down into your new addition, particularly if you plan on plastering or decorating the wall inside. To prevent this, a cavity tray is installed.

The cavity tray should be installed first, and it's always best to use a proprietary remedial tray that can be installed in pieces as you work across the roof, fixing one sheet at a time. The preformed remedial trays are rigid and stand up in the cavity, leaning against the inner leaf to drain water forwards; if they are to work well and keep your conservatory below them dry, they need to overlap and have an upstand at the free end to prevent water cascading off inside the cavity. They also need to have weep-holes for drainage in the perp joints of the occasional brick, and little plastic fillers can be bought to fit these. The positioning of trays is important: they are usually two brick courses high, but must discharge out over the top of the flashing material. Some come with lead flashing attached to achieve this more easily.

Flashings

This element is the cover over the joint of roof and wall. Obviously it can't be dressed down until roof is on, but the brickwork can be cut to allow for it. A disc-cutting tool will grind out a groove in a masonry joint for the flashing to be inserted, as it can't simply be face-fixed to the wall.

Flashings come in a variety of materials. Lead is the traditional one and Code 4 is the recommended thickness, but this can be difficult to dress down over polycarbonate. It has the advantage that you can pin the flashing into the chase (with lead wedges) now and keep it folded up out of the way to be dressed down

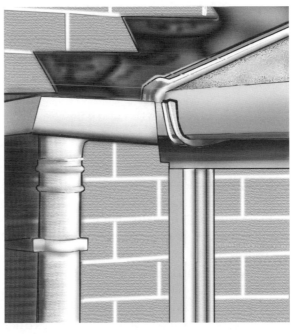

Stepped flashing seals the roof edge to the wall

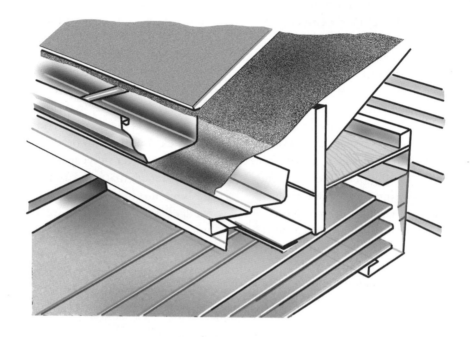

Where polycarbonate roofs run beneath an existing roof,
fixing to the fascia is possible with aluminium fittings

later. Normally it's hammered down with a rubber mallet.

Self-adhesive bitumen-based flashings stick well to plastic, but I would still insert them into a chase in the wall as they don't stick to brickwork so well. These are used all too commonly in conservatory roofs, not always successfully. A good width that will dress over the joint by 100–150 mm either side is needed. A preformed plastic flashing that has been specially designed for use with a polycarbonate roof is preferred.

Fascia fixings

On a bungalow, your conservatory roof may have to connect with the existing fascia, rather than the wall below it. In these cases, aluminium extruded fittings can be fixed to the bottom of the fascia to support the roof sheets. The polycarbonate sheets will run in beneath the eaves, where they need to be sealed against the wall.

Supports (not self-supporting systems)

If you're using rafters to support your sheets, your glazing bars will run down them and be fully supported along their length, screwed down at 400 mm centres.

If you have purlins, timbers that run horizontally across the roof, you'll need to screw the bottom half of the glazing bar to every purlin and let it span the gap between them. The maximum span you can do this for is 1500 mm, but it makes for a stronger roof if you cut this down and limit the purlin spacings to 1000 mm. You need to use screws with plenty of bite that will sink in to about half the depth of the rafter or purlin. Stainless steel are best to avoid corrosion, but bed them into a dollop of clear silicone mastic to stop rainwater leaking around the hole.

Side trimming

With the glazing bars fixed, the side trims or flashings can now be added. Some trims are pre-drilled to accept screws, with oversize holes to allow for some expansion movement. If you have to drill your own, add 3 mm to the screw diameter to achieve this.

Fixing the sheets

Polycarbonate can be scratched quite easily, and is usually supplied with a protective film attached. Leave this film on for the most part, but peel it back at the ends only, as you need to check that you've got the end with the sealing tape, not the breathable tape, uppermost.

Run a bead of clear silicone mastic along the side flashing (or verge trim) and push the sheet into this and into position. The sheet's other edge and vertical rib should engage with the glazing bar. The sheet needs some careful positioning to allow for thermal expansion, and you should look for a 10 mm gap at the top from the wall and a 3 mm gap at the sides when you fix the side flashing; in fact, apart from the top, that 3 mm gap around all fixings of the sheets is the standard. It helps if you have something to retain the sheet against at the bottom to prevent it from slipping down the roof until you have finished. The side flashing should be fixed before you add the second sheet to the roof.

You can dress the flashing at the top now to this sheet (while you can get at it from the inside), although this is a job that needs to be done in stages, overlapping at each sheet if you don't want to be clambering over the roof when you've finished.

Add the second sheet to the glazing bar and place the cover strip over the two edges; these pieces usually snap-lock into place with a little encouragement from a rubber mallet. They are down fully when the edge seals are pressing firmly against the polycarbonate sheet – it's important that they do to keep the weather out. Once the sheet is down, move up to the flashing for this section and proceed across the roof in this way until you reach the other side. Before this last sheet goes on the other side, the flashing (edge trim) needs to be fixed in place.

GLASS PROPERTIES

Type	Weight	Light transmission	U value
6-mm thick single glazed Georgian-wired	17.1 kg/sq m	90%	4.5
24 mm thick double-glazed + low-e coated (4 toughened + 16 + 4)	19.6 kg/sq m	75%	2.0
28-mm thick low-e coated double-glazed + argon filled cavity (4 toughened + 20 + 4)	19.6 kg/sq m	75%	1.6

DOUBLE-GLAZED GLASS ROOFS

Advantages	Disadvantages
Good thermal insulation	Expensive
Good sound insulation against rainfall and airborne sound	Heavier
Robust material	Needs shading
Remains stable against thermal changes	Seals have 10 years' life expectancy
Secure against burglary	

With the sheets down, cover strips locked and flashings completed, the protective film can be removed from the sheets and they can be given a bit of a clean with soapy water and a sponge. You can't scrub this material with a brush without scratching it, so it pays to give it a regular sponge and hose-down to keep it clear.

Glass roofing

Before the advent of double-glazing, all conservatory roofs were glass. Once glass safety became an issue and BS:6206 arrived, the only suitable glass for roofing became Georgian-wired. As a cast plate it had the obscured finish that allowed it to be used in the windows of public toilets – and that unfortunately is where most people still view it today. Georgian-wired glass is still produced, but more commonly as polished plate glass of fine clarity. Technology has moved onto toughened and laminated safety glass that comes without any apparent difference in its appearance to ordinary glass. And so Georgian-wired has all but disappeared from our homes – and nobody seems to miss it.

Glass above head height can give some people the jitters, and for it to be safely installed there are some basic rules to be observed, the first being how it is to be supported. Glazing bars for most conservatory roofs run down the length of the roof supported on the rafters, and this two-edge system with the panes in one

piece is often all that is needed. If there are unsupported edges at the ends because of the length of the roof slope, these will need to be stepped and flashed (sealed) against windblown rain penetration. The four-edge system of glazing picks up these ends with extra glazing bars so each pane is supported on all sides. With bars horizontally placed across the roof, provision has to be made for drainage, and the system needs some careful design, given the roof pitch and spans of the panes and bars. In any case, patent-glazing systems shouldn't be used below a pitch of 15°.

Toughened glass used for roofing should be of the heat-soaked variety, which the makers can guarantee against the risk of spontaneous fracture. Ordinary toughened glass fractures into a mosaic of tiny pieces that in vertical panes mostly stay put. But in a roof with gravity working against it, these pieces can shower down and cause injury to people below; spontaneous fracturing is not something you want to experience beneath a glass roof. So how does it occur? Apparently there are some types of defects in the glass that can give rise to it, and a number of these, ironically enough, are specifically related to the toughening process. Adding nickel sulphide to glass used to be a major problem in the 1960s, and still is if the annealed glass from which it is made is of less than excellent quality. More commonly, glass breaks because it has been badly installed or mishandled, and these days, with strict quality control procedures in the manufacturing process, material flaws are rare.

Heat-soaking glass eliminates the risk of defects at the edges or from nickel sulphide, by exposing the material to high temperature levels for timed periods.

Self-cleaning glass

You also need to give some thought to how the glass will be cleaned. Good ladder access around the perimeter of the roof is essential to avoid the need to crawl or walk on it.

If you've ever noticed how the water droplets on a newly waxed and polished car are rounder and spaced further apart than those on a dirty car, you've understood the concept of self-cleaning glass. It isn't rocket science, and now, in addition to glass, polycarbonate sheeting can be purchased with this coating factory-applied.

I first saw this on BBC's *Tomorrow's World* many years ago, where it was described as a revolutionary treatment for windscreen glass that the rain would simply stream off, practically eliminating the need for wipers. It doesn't seem to have happened for cars, but hydrophobic coatings (as they are now known) have been with us for window glazing for quite a while. They haven't exactly

revolutionised anything, but they do help to keep the glass clean in locations where it would quickly become grubby – where traffic film, tree sap or bird populations are high and the average window-cleaning regime is not going to be enough. Hydrophobic coatings are not going to replace window cleaners, but by reducing the surface tension of the glass. they can stretch out the intervals between cleaning. The rain itself helps to wash the window or roof sheet.

Roof ridges and capping

The capping on a 'glazed' roof is the weathering cap that covers the joints in the glazed panels; with polycarbonate roofs this is always PVC-u and quite often a bit on the chunky side. Some conservatory manufacturers have taken the trouble of slimming down the rafter pieces and caps on their Victorian style range to mimic the style of the era.

The capping system has been taken on one step further with ventilated ridges and hips that provide exhaust ventilation through weather-resistance slots covered by insect mesh, and although these vents aren't large enough to compensate for an opening rooflight, for example, they do provide passive background ventilation on a permanent and secure basis. The vents are controllable with slide close covers, but the point is to leave them open for seasons at a time. Trickle vents, as they are sometimes known, have been required in new-build windows since 1990, and adopt the same design to achieve a permanently vented roof space that will help to keep condensation at bay and the room cool. However, venting at a draught-free high level like this is good for us but not so great for plants. For them, introducing fresh air at a lower level and letting it out through the roof is more helpful.

In aluminium systems the rafters are capped by glazing bars (again in aluminium) that can be painted to the colour of your choice. The great advantage of aluminium framing in general is that if supplied in its

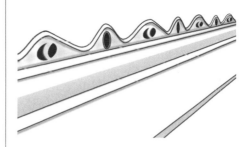

Crested ridge fitting

factory-finish state it can all be painted with an appropriate paint system to your own choice of colour, creating a unique appearance.

To make life easier in the manufacturing, adjustable pitch ridges

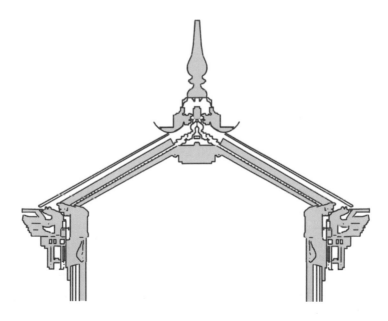

Cross-section through decorative roof finial and eaves beams

are often made that can cope with the typical low pitches of 15°, 20°, 25° and 30° that are common to most conservatories.

Ridges are, for the most part, one of two designs: the plain cap ridge or the 'Victorian' ridge of decorative pointy detailing that terminates in an even more decorative and pointy finial piece. This style aims to emulate the Gothic Revival period of the Victorian era. In a way it tries to make something of a silk purse out of a sow's ear and succeeds, so you can see why it is so popular.

Glazing systems

When a lightweight polycarbonate roof material is used, the rafters are often omitted in small conservatories, and the glazing bars that support the sheeting act in their absence as a kind of 'self-supporting' system. In a lean-to conservatory, a wall plate section of PVC-u or aluminium is secured to the existing wall of the home, and a proprietary eaves beam does the same job at the eaves end. Between them span the glazing bars, but only up to a point. 4 m is the usual considered maximum span for this, the most basic form of roof structure. Both the eaves beam and wall plate are rebated to house the polycarbonate sheets in their standard thicknesses, and at the sides of the roof (the verges) end bars cap the edge of the sheets.

If PVC-u doesn't sound durable or strong enough for your liking, the same elements are available in aluminium, usually with a white or brown factory-applied finish. And if that doesn't do it for you, timber rafters can be installed in a traditional roof to support the aluminium glazing bars complete with PVC capping. With this construction, much greater spans can be achieved, and the rafter tables opposite give you an idea of these, given the dead weight of the material and allowing for some snow loads. Snow-loading is normally designed into all roof structures in the UK, but how much you allow for depends on your location.

Traditional rafters

Because the roof structure is on show, the timber sizes are shown here as finished (PAR – planed all round) timber, rather than the usual sawn material used for rafters. This can be painted, stained or varnished as required. Otherwise the timbers shown are assumed to be stress-graded C16 (SC3), the industry standard structural grade.

With traditional lean-to roofs, the rafters have to be supported on the existing wall, and this is done by either building in the timbers individually to cut-out pockets in the wall, or by securing a wall plate to the wall using expansion or resin-anchor bolts and nailing the rafter ends to it. The plate need only be a similar size to the rafter and can be levelled to ensure a perfect roof level before

Rafter size (PAR)	Centres	Single -Glazing	Double -glazing	Polycarbonate
50 x 75 mm	400 mm	2.50	1.75	3.50
	600 mm	2.25	1.50	3.0
50 x 100 mm	400 mm	3.25	2.50	4.25
	600 mm	3.0	2.25	3.75
50 x 125 mm	400 mm	3.75	3.0	5.0
	600 mm	3.25	2.75	4.5
50 x 150 mm	400 mm	4.75	3.75	6.0
	600 mm	4.25	3.25	5.25

NOTE: The maximum spans shown are measured along the slope and are for roof pitches of up to 30°. Greater spans can be used for steeper roofs.

being fixed into place. It also has the advantage of being able to take up differences in the plane of the wall, and any bulges, bumps and depressions can be packed out behind the plate so long as it is adequately fixed. The bolts themselves have a propensity to accept relatively high shear loads and do not need to be spaced too close together. Bolt manufacturers display the loading capacity of their bolts in this respect, and you can thus calculate how many you need by dividing it into half the total load of the roof (half because the other half is supported on the frame at the eaves).

Total roof area 16 sq m x 0.5

= 8 sq m

multiplied by

Frame and roof sheets dead weight (of 24 mm

double-glazing) = 22 kg/sq m

or 0.22 kN/sq m

+ snow (live) load allowance

= 0.6 kN/sq m

equals a total roof load to all bolts of

8 x (0.22 + 0.6) = 6.56 kN

Ordering structural timber

There are specific requirements for timber used in construction, particularly in the case of structural members, whether they are used in roofs, floors or walls.

Grading

There are many strength grades for timber, ranging from the weakest softwood to the strongest hardwood, but only two are used for structural softwood – C16 and C24. You should ensure that roof timbers in sun lounges and garden rooms are at least 'DRY' graded: this doesn't mean they will actually turn up dry, but that their moisture content is limited to a maximum of 24 per cent; this means they shouldn't turn up saturated. Every piece of structural timber must be stamp-marked to say what stress grade it is, among other information to say whether it is DRY or KN (kiln-dried). You should quote KN grading for conservatory roof timbers, because these may be subjected to rapid drying out beneath the glazed roof, and if they have a lot of moisture content to lose, this will cause them to shrink and split.

Preservative treatment

This should be requested on ordering as a pressure/vacuum treatment for protection against fungal and insect attack. Timber treatment can be done yourself with some products.

Although CCA (chromated copper arsenic) is now banned from use in dwellings, it is important to know that all timber preservatives contain harmful chemicals, and any on-site treatment of timber should be done with extreme care and protective clothing on. In any event, applying it with a brush or sprayer isn't the same as pressure-treating it, which penetrates the wood to a much greater extent.

Selection

Before accepting the delivery of any timber, check it for splits, shakes, knots and any bent or warped lengths, and reject anything unsuitable before signing the delivery ticket or paying. The quality of timber varies, and it isn't unusual for some of it to be so low it isn't suitable for use. To be sure your lumber has arrived from sustainable and managed forests, look for the trademark of the FSC (Forest Stewardship Council.)

Finishing touches

It is often worth adding some detailing to the eaves or ridges of roofs; timber mouldings have always been available for cornicing or dado rails. Most of these will serve well as coving details for the inside of the eaves beam beneath the roof, but if you can't bear to include real timber or MDF in your plastic 'paint-free' room, some of the plastic extruders now also produce fancy bits to personalise your new space. I am given to understand that by 2003, one manufacturer had managed to offload 40 km of the stuff to style-hungry consumers.

Given that you can't decorate a glazed roof much beyond hanging a ceiling fan from the ridge, any styling along the line of the eaves is a focal point that is much appreciated.

Lead coverings

For small bay garden rooms, orangeries or additions to Georgian homes, lead is often the best alternative to glass for the roof material, as the two materials always go well together.

Lead is a soft and malleable metal that can be dressed to glass, masonry and timber, making it as common

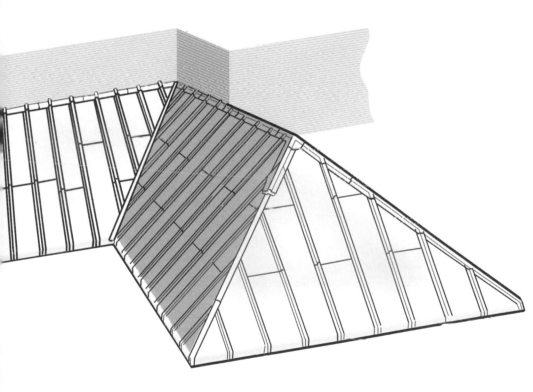

Lead-covered hip-ended roof with rolls running down the slope

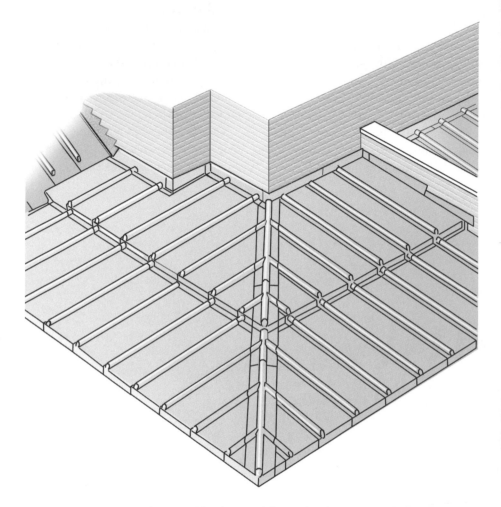

A stepped lead-covered flat roof with rolls

today as it was centuries ago. It does have a nasty habit when it's new of leaching out carbonate when it gets rained on, and staining anything below it white; this is called patination, and the only way to prevent it is to seal the metal with patination oil as soon as the lead is installed. Because it expands and shrinks beneath the sun, lead has to be laid in relatively small pieces; on roofs, this means cutting it into bays and finding a way of joining them. The method of choice is often the lead roll, which you may have

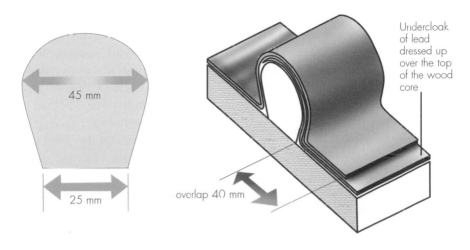

Undercloak of lead dressed up over the top of the wood core

45 mm

25 mm

overlap 40 mm

Wood core rolls for lead covering with overlaps

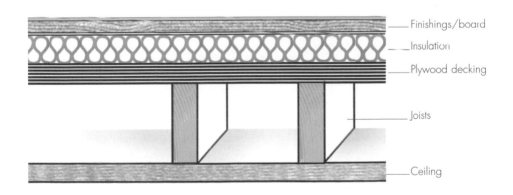

Finishings/board

Insulation

Plywood decking

Joists

Ceiling

Insulation board sandwiched in a warm roof construction

147

seen running down the slope of a roof towards the gutter. Not just functional but decorative as well, rolls have a wood core shaped like a handrail that is screwed down to the decking material, with the lead from each side dressed up and lapped over it. The lead is normally extended 40 mm beyond on the top layer (overcloak) to weather it against rain. While the bottom layer (undercloak) is nailed to the roll, the overcloak isn't.

Because lead can be dressed over glass rather neatly, it can be jointed with it, which means that you can have the top half of a pitched roof covered by lead sheet and the lower half glazed. There is no other material that this works so well in as lead, and even when the solid half is tiles or covered by slates, the joining of the two materials can only be done effectively in leadwork.

The size of the bays is determined by the code thickness of the lead – the thicker it is the larger the bay size, and Codes 6, 7 and 8 are mostly used in sheet roofing. Laying lead sheet is a skill that comes with training and experience, and when it's done by a skilled tradesman it looks impressive. When it's not, it looks terrible.

A lead sheet roof can be applied to a pitched roof or flat roof; the only difference comes with the lapping of joints to maintain the weather resistance at different pitches. To keep the wind from lifting the roof up at the joints, clips made of copper or stainless steel are used. These two materials are compatible with lead, and you should stick to either of them for fixing leadwork in place. Nails can be used to pin lead sheets down to a timber-boarded deck (like plywood), while the clip holds the lapped joint in place and is used for roof pitches over 30°. Under this the wind uplift increases, so some extra jointing precautions are necessary, and a clip made from a strip of Code 4 or 5 lead is welded along the joint continuously for each bay. It's common practice to stagger the continuous clip joints for each bay so that you don't have to wrestle with the added problem of jointing them up at the meeting of bays.

Flat roofs

Flat roof structures are the simplest of all roofs to build, but perhaps the least economical. The joists will only span so far, and with the load on flat roofs equalling two-thirds of that on a floor, they remain quite large sections of timber.

There is also one major drawback, which comes from insulating and ventilating flat-roof structures. Lagging them between the joists with glass fibre is no longer an option, as the depth of insulation and ventilation required prevents this from being possible. To achieve the necessary standard, which is reduced from that

LEAD-COVERED FLAT ROOF JOIST SPANS

Stress grade	C16 grade	C16 grade	C24 grade	C24 grade
Spacings in mm →	400 mm	600 mm	400 mm	600 mm
Joist section sizes ↓	Maximum spans in metres		Maximum spans in metres	
50 x 100	1.89	1.77	1.99	1.86
50 x 125	2.53	2.37	2.62	2.43
50 x 150	3.19	2.97	3.27	3.01
50 x 175	3.81	3.47	3.91	3.53
50 x 200	4.48	3.97	4.56	4.03
50 x 225	5.09	4.47	5.15	4.52

needed in pitched roofs lagged at ceiling tie level, you must look to insulating with high-performing materials such as polyurethane foam board. Some of these are factory-bonded to ply decking to fix directly onto the joists, but often the ply is very thin (6 mm) and lacks robustness, so you might prefer to form your own with a thicker (18 mm) deck.

The alternative to this form of warm roof is a cold roof using thinner multi-laminate foil type insulation that is made up of several layers of aluminium foil, phenolic foam and thin quilt, which together are less than 25 mm thick but achieve excellent insulation values similar to 200 mm of glass fibre. You will need to ventilate the void between the insulation and the deck with vents fitted at the fascia to afford a cross-flow of air.

Spans in excess of these will need to be justified by structural design calculations, and may well need supporting beams to carry them.

If you plan to use your flat roof as a deck or balcony it becomes a floor, and floor joist tables should be referred to. If your plan takes you one step further, to using the deck for roof gardening and laying floor slabs, for example, you will need the services of a structural engineer to design the joists against the additional load. The maximum dead load allowed here is 1 kN/sq m.

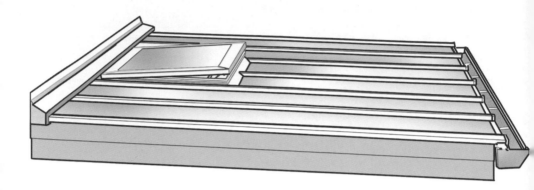

An opening roof vent

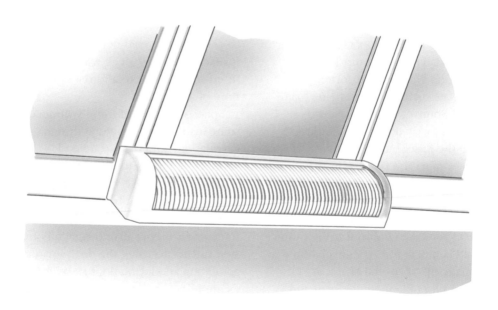

A proprietary roof ventilator

Ventilation and shade

With a transparent roof and mostly glazed walls, your conservatory has a tremendous ability to absorb solar heat. This will be its main attraction for you in spring and autumn, a place in the sun but out of the cold wind. In summer, however, it can very quickly become unusable.

It is vital that you consider the aspect that yours will have, and what shade, if any, it will enjoy. East- and west facing conservatories are ideal, but ones exposed to the south will mean designing in some shade and good ventilation: tinted glass, for example, can be used in the roof to reflect the power of the sun, or you may decide to limit the extent of glazing in proportion to a tiled roof. What you don't want to do is end up with a room that you can only use for half of the year – not the half when the garden is at its best.

Airflow is important too, and a roof vent will allow warm air to be exhausted out as well as relieving wind pressure inside the room that occurs when a window or door is open. Lightweight structures such as conservatories can be damaged by wind uplift, so a roof vent allows the air to flow through your conservatory, not simply into it.

CHAPTER EIGHT

Furnishing and finishing

Floor finishings

Your choice of floor covering should largely be determined by the use you intend to put the new room to: the conservatory sitting areas of residential homes furnished with comfy armchairs are often carpeted, but for most domestic conservatories and sun lounges, a hardwearing finish from tiles or laminate is better. With tiling you have the distinct advantage of being able to splash the occasional drop of water (or bucketful, in my case) when tending plants. With your new glazed room giving you the chance to enjoy the garden from inside, the use of natural stone floor slabs is perfect to enhance the transition. The primary stones used in floor tiles are limestone, sandstone, slate, granite and marble.

Limestone and sandstone

These two are sedimentary rocks that are porous in nature and formed in layers. They are easy to cut and relatively soft, but this does mean that they can be bought in a variety of finishes, from bush-hammered to flame-finished or honed. With its whiteish colour, limestone can sometimes look a little cold and you may have to spend some time sourcing a richer shade that errs more towards cream or buff tones. It reflects sunlight tremendously well beneath a glass roof, and if you have

a large floor to cover, sunglasses might be compulsory, as the reflected light from it can be blinding. Limestone is made up of tiny shells of prehistoric sea life, and its durability is directly related to the size of the open pores: the finer the pores, the less durable the stone.

Sandstones vary a great deal more in colour, from the almost pure white material of Egypt, particularly the ancient West Bank of Luxor, to the deep red and brown found in parts of England, such as Kent and Devon. Whatever you use, there will be some variation from slab to slab in both texture and colour, inherent in any natural material. This makes it essential to lay out plenty of tiles at a time, if not actually all of them, and see how they can best be mixed. If you don't take the trouble to mix them, you can end up with patches or large squares of one finish contrasting with larger areas of another, which will look as though you under-ordered the first time and had to use another material to finish the job. Blending through any variations in shade with a bit more subtlety removes this effect and lets you appreciate the variation.

Because limestone and sandstone are porous you might want to consider impregnating or sealing them, but this can also have an effect on the finish, so try it on some samples first. Unless you can guarantee that somebody isn't going to knock over a glass of red wine, sealing this kind of stone is essential, but don't let yourself become obsessed with the imperfections of the surface. Yes, tiles do sometimes become pitted and holes can appear, but this is part of the charm of natural stone, and if you're going to fill every flaw with grout maybe you should choose ceramic tiles instead. Before you apply any solution, make sure that the tiles are spotlessly clean and dry first. If you do need to clean any, specialised stone-cleaning agents should be used. Both of these sedimentary rocks require a thickness in slabs of at least 75 mm.

For outdoor use, the chemical composition of sandstone will determine its weather-resistance, not the nature of the sand that it bonds together. Where calcium carbonate is the bonding chemical, acid rain can rapidly deteriorate it, and sandstone is tested for durability by being dipped in a weak sulphuric acid.

Slate

When we think of slate, most of us picture the roof of a Victorian house, but slate can be obtained in a wide variety of colours, and when it's used for flooring, slabs are cut in a much greater thickness. Welsh slate is still mined and can be ordered from source; even here, the colours will vary from one mine to another, with purples and greys through to near black, but slate is widely available from other countries, too, notably Spain, India, Turkey and China. African slate can even be obtained in almost pure black, veined with coloured minerals for a luxurious touch. Westmoreland slate is green or orangey, and sometimes both.

Slate isn't porous by nature – quite the reverse, hence its use on and as damp-proof coursing. It does mark and scratch, however, and is still worth protecting if you can avoid giving it a shiny wet-look coating. Regular oiling is needed. It does have the tremendous advantage of being capable of perfect flatness (hence its use in snooker tables), and if you have a dining table and chairs to set in your conservatory, they will appreciate this fact immeasurably.

Marble

Marble invariably comes from Italy, but it can be imported from other countries, and as well as spelling out the words 'sheer luxury' on the floor, it is tremendously hardwearing and a joy to clean; visit the lobby of any decent hotel to see what it looks like. In laying it, you have to have some respect for the veins. It will prove impossible to join them up, but if they generally head in the same direction it looks right. When they don't or when the tiler has tried to follow a vein for a few tiles before giving up is where it looks wrong, and you'll feel the

153

dilemma of the tiler every time you look at it. Being igneous and metamorphic rocks, granite and marble can be used in much thinner slabs.

Granite

Granite is the ultimate in hardwearing stone floors, and comes in shades of blue, grey to black and then brown and fawn, even flecked with pink, but with natural materials being so popular now, even designer stones are available as something you could call 'customised nature', from pebbles set in clear resin and cut into slabs to porcelain with a metallic finish.

Walls

I'm surprised at how many conservatory owners choose to retain the facing bricks of their existing home for the inside back wall of the conservatory, rather than plastering and decorating them. Brickwork of the right quality and appearance can look good inside, but much of it isn't ideal. Modern bricks, particularly the sand-faced flettons used for homes in the 1960s, 1970s and 1980s are a bit rough-faced, and once you've rubbed your elbow against them a few times the desire to plaster over them will be irresistible.

However, a smooth-faced brick, a red stock worn smooth over many decades, is a different story. The aged quality and warm colour of the brick face, together with a smooth and kind-on-the-flesh finish, can make a perfect backdrop for a new garden room. Bricks do have the great advantage of absorbing the sun's heat and releasing it steadily through the evening and night, so you could find yourself sitting out there after dark when the garden is chilly, still basking in the day's warmth radiating from the walls.

Bricks that aren't pretty to look at can always be painted white or cream to reflect the light, or shades of blue, orange or green to absorb it. With the unique status that a conservatory has, colours that you might not use indoors could be perfectly at home in this chimera zone that is half outdoors and half in: that rear wall rendered and painted Moroccan blue or tangerine orange could create the exotic atmosphere of North Africa, for example, while in an English garden, green prevails, and any shade of green paint will create the illusion of being entirely outside.

Décor and colour

If you go for it nowhere else in your home, the conservatory is the place to be bold with colour. Here, in this twilight zone betwixt in and out, daylight abounds and sunlight streams in to bring life and radiance to the colour of your choice. What I'm trying to say is, leave the lid on the magnolia.

You have perhaps only one full-height wall to decorate, so why not

UNROLLING THE COLOUR WHEEL

Toning shades are the shades from one colour through the segment to the centre from the outer edge. If you chose any colour on the outside of the wheel, adding white to it in varying degrees will gradually take you to the centre – each is a tone along the way.

Contrasting colours are a lot more mysterious. These colours can be found on opposite sides of the wheel and they are for some reason the ones that work to complement each other, rather than arguing all the time: orange and blue, green and brown, for example. You won't find black and white on a colour wheel, but if you could, they would be opposite each other.

Harmony colours are a bit easier to understand. The segments sit beside each other on the wheel and offer similar temperatures: orange and yellow, blue and purple. In many ways they are naturally suited alongside each other as they appear in the spectrum.

make it a feature wall colour-wise, and if you have tiling or soft furnishings to dress in with it, use a colour wheel to find successful combinations.

Colour and mood

I don't think there are too many rooms in the house where I could live with the colour of violet on the walls – maybe on one wall and in one small room if it was assuaged with some cream or green to balance its cooling effect. In a conservatory, however, violet, the colour of so many flowers, positively glows in the sunshine and lives happily against the green backdrop of a garden.

Orange creates an exotic feel that warms the room in winter when the sunlight is watery. Take a leap of faith away from the soft end of orange, past those peach shades that are for bedrooms, and go with real orange or terracotta for the feeling of warmth and some added zest.

Technically you can't do better than blue in a small, well-lit room such as your average conservatory. Blue pushes back the walls, making the space seem bigger (the exact opposite of red or orange, which appear to make them cosier but smaller), and if you go for a deep blue rather than a pale blue sky, it can bring a touch of the Mediterranean to your home. Finding the exact shade of blue that suits you is a challenge: you might not want it to look like a mid-range common blue and you might not want it to be too close to navy and darkness. Blues that edge towards green and are almost but not quite turquoise or blues that hint towards violet are for me the perfect ones. They have a quality that reflects nature at its most glorious in a coral sea or the feathers of a peacock, but to achieve them you will have to start with a well prepared undercoat.

In trying to reproduce the radiance of light in their paintings, artists sometimes use a technique known as underglazing. They prepare the canvas with a glaze that is a mixture of varnish, linseed oil and turpentine, and then paint over it. When the light falls on the picture, some of it reflects back from the glaze beneath the oil colours, giving them a luminance that they would otherwise lack. Now I admit that I haven't heard of anyone doing this or anything similar to it in home decorating – not even on the most radical of TV makeover shows – but it occurs to me that it could work just as well using a silicone coating beneath a compatible paint. Silicone solutions are designed to cover brickwork to increase its weather-resistance, and you will need to find out what type of paint (if any) will overcoat them, but it but it could be worth experimenting with.

Alternative linings

If plaster and paint are not to your taste and suggest a bit too much maintenance, some materials can be used to line the walls and be left untouched thereafter. One that might surprise you is cellular PVC-u: the same material used in soffit boards and external cladding has been developed in a range of colours and finishings for internal use. Metal, marble and wood effects all come in this tongued-and-grooved board form that is maintenance-free and wipe clean. I've seen whole rooms – not conservatories – done in this, and they look a little like hotel bathrooms, but in a sun lounge with less wall area and plenty of shade, it could be the answer. In a conservatory with plenty of heat, it may well buckle.

Natural stone is also being sold now with adhesives for wall tiling. It seems bizarre at first that anybody would want to patio an inside wall, but if you go back to the 1970s, you'll remember how cool it was to glue artificial stone cladding on the outside wall of your home. At least, some people thought so. Natural stone cut into manageably smaller squares for walls is a lot more classy, especially when used on just one wall (a feature wall) or dressed up a dwarf wall from the floor tiled in the same materials.

If you have a patient tiler and are prepared to spend a bit more, having square tiles laid to a diamond on the diagonal (corner to vertical corner) is very effective and takes away that shrinking perspective you get when you lay tiles square.

BS:8298 is the standard for natural stone cladding and lining, and this is

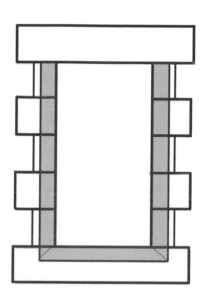

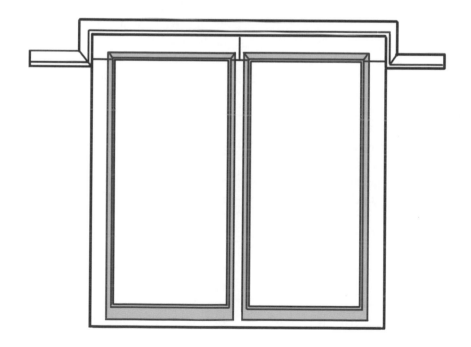

Resin stone surrounds can be surface-fixed or built-in
to display windows in garden rooms

the code of practice for both design and installation if you intend to employ a tiling firm to carry out the work. Make sure you have their written agreement to comply with this standard.

Decking outside

Perhaps it's a happy coincidence, but conservatory building and deck building seem to have grown together in popularity. In many ways, decking seemed like a fad that would pass by soon and allow patios back into our hearts and rear gardens. Maybe later. The late 1990s saw the arrival of decking in the UK, thanks to TV garden shows, and it has continued to be popular.

Timber looks great and is always a pleasure to work with, so perhaps it isn't surprising that in 2004, with over 500,000 decks formed in our gardens the domestic decking market was said to be worth £35,000,000 to its manufacturers. Given that most of us have only owned a deck for a few years, we don't really know what their life expectancy is going to be. One thing is for sure – it will have a lot to do with the quality of the materials and design, plus the regularity of maintenance thrown in. Our weather is one of the reasons why decks, like patios, are so popular. They create a 'dry zone' from the garden into the home, where we can walk or sit with our feet out of the mud, but it's this wet weather that is likely to reduce

their longevity if they aren't carefully constructed. In summer the hot sun can bleach and split timber making handrails untouchable and boards curl up, but in wet weather they can be slippery and destined to rot if not properly treated and drained.

Starting with the base, decks in Australia are platforms that allow wildlife to harbour beneath them, and Australia has plenty of wildlife that you specifically don't want harbouring beneath your home, so keeping a deck on the deck has a distinct advantage there. Sure, we have rats and hedgehogs in this country that would be pleased to make a home in a sub-deck area, but we also have the more important problem of wet ground, ground that is wet for months on end, and wood and wet ground are not happy companions. Most of our decks are therefore slightly raised.

On some homes, steeply sloping garden levels have made deck construction almost essential if a level sitting area is going to be found, but that has meant building a framework of braced stilts that can give homes the unique look of a Filipino fishing village. The deck to your conservatory needs only to be separated from the earth by a few centimetres if you have the choice. Achieving this isn't difficult if you consider it to be a framework of timber bearers or joists raised up on concrete foundation pads or stub posts, over which the

Decking needs to be robust and durable and that includes the balustrading.
Look for these qualities over appearance – the bottom picture has them

boards can be laid. If the timbers are strong enough to withstand the load the contact with the ground can be minimal but in most cases you won't be using railway sleepers.

Regularised timber has a stress grade and sizing that means it will need to be deep if it is to span far without deflecting, and I prefer the method of haunching these bearers onto a lean concrete mix for most of their length. As anyone who has ever concreted a fence post into the ground and watched it rot over the following few years knows, concrete takes up ground water and holds it, so it is essential that these bearers are large and effectively treated with preservative. Since they aren't going to be on show, they don't have to be pretty, and you might be able to find lengths of seasoned and hard secondhand timbers that can be freshly treated. Species such as deal, hemlock and oak are perfect, but if you are buying softwood from the timber merchants, it is worth paying the extra to have it pressure-treated beforehand. If you can't avoid having a high-rise deck, steps down to the garden should have risers no greater than 220 mm and treads no less than 220 mm. Have nothing steeper than 42° in pitch, and you will have a safe stair. I recomment you look to using solid 100 x 100 mm newel posts to help make the balustrading rigid, and keep the top rail 1100 mm high.

Blinds

Although some variation in style exists, the material choice for blinds is relatively limited.

Standard pleated blinds come in all the colours of the rainbow plus a couple of hundred more. Depending on the colour, the heat reflection can be anything up to about 80 per cent, but if you choose dark colours, heat absorption is far more likely. Special solar-reflective fabrics that are ultra-lightweight and can be easily wiped clean of dust are available. Material such as this is usually quoted as having a solar reflection of 85 per cent, slightly (but only slightly) better than standard white blinds.

As a third choice, pinoleum can be thought of as a traditional heritage material, since it has been made in France for over a century. It is woven from thin strips of wood to create a wonderfully translucent blind that lets dappled sunlight through. I think this is the best material for plants, and it complements rattan and wicker furniture, but I'm not sure about its effectiveness for keeping the room cool. It certainly looks stylish and is usually very durable, but it must be a safe harbour for dust and a devil to clean.

For blinds to work to their full potential, they need to have a high reflectance value and allow only a small percentage of light through.

Inevitably, some of the light and heat will be absorbed by the blind, and each material has different values in these three aspects.

Pleated blinds are the simplest of all, but can only be fitted to windows and doors, not roofs. They are operated by string pull cords, so you can end up with a lot of cord dangling between each window frame, and the potential exists for the things to snag and tangle up. Usually they are made from polyester fabric, which has some lightfast characteristics to prevent the colour fading, and should be made to order to ensure they fit properly. Typically this material will reflect about three-quarters of the light, absorb about one-fifth of the total, and only let a tiny amount penetrate through when the blinds are closed.

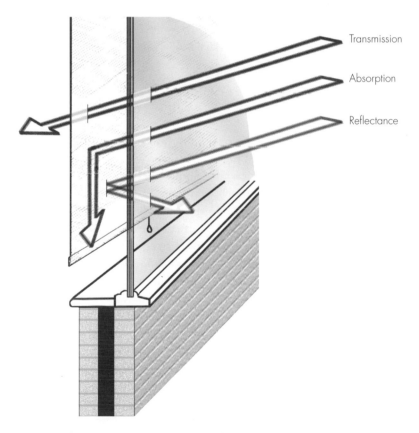

Transmission

Absorption

Reflectance

Blinds serve three purposes to a greater or lesser extent depending on the material

BLINDS

Transmission values relate the amount of both heat and light that can pass through a material. Even glass has a transmission value of less than 100 per cent, but for blinds you might want to look for a low percentage here which would indicate a high performing shade.

Reflectance should be the highest proportion of all by far, if the blind is to work well and keep the room cooler on summer days and warmer at night. It is the amount of heat and light reflected back by the blind. Some materials are specially lined to achieve high percentages here, and these should perform the best when it comes to keeping the room at an even temperature.

Absorption is the bit that's left over. Some heat isn't reflected back or allowed to pass through the blind, but is absorbed by the material itself. Some blinds may have a lining on the inside designed to trap heat, and this will help to keep the room cool during the day, although the stored heat will be released later when the conservatory is cooling down. Soft furnishings like settees and armchairs will do the same.

Roller blinds or panel blinds can be made to fit everywhere, roof panels included. Made from polyester cotton, which has a lower reflectance value (around 60 per cent) and higher transmission (of about 20 per cent), they are well suited to conservatories with plants, where they filter down the direct sunlight without blocking too much of it out; this is often achieved by using aluminised fabric, which has an aluminium backing that bounces back the glare and heat of the sun.

Vertical strip blinds are very effective for keeping in heat, particularly when the material is coated on both faces to keep them hanging straight and not twisted. Some can be fitted with control systems that eliminate the pull cords. Depending on the material, they can reflect back 60–75 per cent of heat as they overlap when closed to keep the warmth in. They do tend to absorb less than most other types.

Some materials have been created to reflect heat and light, thus shading the conservatory much more efficiently. If you have a south-facing aspect or use the room for dining or socialising in, you may want to keep it as cool as you can in summer. Reflectance of up to 80 per cent can be found in some roof blinds.

Drapes

It is difficult with any blinds to escape the office look if they are comprehensively installed, and drapes create a much softer appearance.

Subtle shading can be introduced with soft muslin and voile, in the form of drapes, or from the roof, sailcloth style. They add some shade to plants and people, but do little to reflect heat out of the conservatory, being unfitted and hanging well beneath the roof glazing. They do, however, look tremendously romantic and give a conservatory a much softer and relaxed appearance than blinds can ever do. Because they aren't going to shade you (or your plants), you might need to use them in conjunction with freestanding timber shutters – tall, louvred shutter boards (in pairs hinged together) that you can move with the sun are ideal, particularly when you paint the outer face white. The material to make shutters is commonly available from DIY stores, and they can look very Victorian if you have the appropriate style of conservatory.

Glazed-in blinds

Although I have not seen these used in external glazing in the domestic sector, they are becoming quite common in office screening, where they consist of a double-glazed window or partition with a louvred shutter blind fitted within the air gap between the glass panes. Operated with sliding control knobs fitted in the frame, the blinds can be totally or partially closed at the flick of the wrist, and because they are glazed in, they blank out the window to 100 per cent effectiveness.

When used in external glazing, the solar reflection can be very high, since the radiation is bounced back out before it reaches the inner pane of glass, never reaching the inside air of the room. Because insulated double-glazing relies on a sealed air gap to be free from condensation, a secondary gap (triple-glazing) for the blinds is necessary, and the cost is high. As already established, fully fitted blinds aren't cheap either, and with this technology, added insulation is also provided to both heat and sound, so glazed-in blinds could become worth having.

Furnishings

I wouldn't recommend too much soft furnishing in a conservatory; for one thing, the long-term exposure to sunlight will soon fade the material, and for another, the risk of heat damage is quite real. The sun is a powerful thing, and its energy through glass can be focused to the extreme. As I write this, somebody is busy trying to clear the fire damage from their new and completed bedroom extension. It's only March, but it seems that they had left a shaving mirror on the windowsill, and while they were out the sun bounced off of it with laser-like qualities and

Bamboo, cane and rattan furniture

set fire to the curtains and bed. They came home to find the house full of smoke and the new extension at the centre of it.

Cane or rattan furniture with cushions fitted or scattered is ideal for conservatories, and woven seagrass is much more durable to exposure and surprisingly comfortable, even without a shower of cushions. Rattan can be harvested from the vine after it's grown a metre or two, which allows it to regrow, making it a potentially sustainable material. But since it usually comes from tropical forests, it is also worth checking the origins with the supplier.

Bamboo is a clump-forming grass that is easily cultivated. You might even grow your own in here, which leads us to the last section of the book, my favourite subject for conservatories.

Plants for the conservatory

Whether you want to create a plant haven in your conservatory, with earth beds richly planted with exotic species, or just have a pot or two alive with something fashionable from the world of indoor gardening, you will need to select your species carefully if they are to flourish.

Oddly enough, most house plants won't like it out there. They have been cultivated from the kind of tropical species that enjoy low-light levels and a constant year-round warmth. Conservatories tend to have high light levels and dramatic variations in temperature that won't be enjoyed by glossy, green-leafed house plants, such as Philodendrons, Monstera (Swiss cheese plant) and Ficus (rubber plant). It's a shame, because these species are all good architectural plants that can be bought at a good size cheaply and make for a permanent green feature.

But you can do much better than them – with the summer extended, sunlight and heat magnified, you can grow sub-tropical species that burst into richly coloured flowers and fragrances, plants that couldn't survive outside or in most rooms, but will flourish in the ecosystem of a glazed room. Not only can they tolerate low temperatures in the winter, 5–10° C above freezing, but this rest period is essential for them if they are to flourish and bloom the next summer, when temperatures can soar beyond 30° C. So what are these perfect conservatory plants?

Bougainvillaea, Nerium (oleander), Pelargonium, Jasmine, Hibiscus, Passiflora and Daturas would be my favourites, but look for any plant that enjoys direct sunlight at least for part of the day and a cool restful winter where only a little watering, if any, is needed. Many of them are natural climbers and can be trained up the house wall or conservatory frame, such as Jasmine and Bougainvillaea, and after a few years of growth you will have to control them with seasonal pruning. Others, such as Nerium, are shrubs that will form into a large bushy specimen given a large enough tub and these can be used to decorate a large conservatory – its flowers are fragrant reds and pinks that keep coming all summer and autumn.

Others, such as Passiflora (passionflower) and Plumbago, are basically vines and can be trained along wires fixed to the rafters or walls – you could include Manettia (firecracker plant) in this category for a red flower instead of blue. If you'd rather not have something that crawls all over the place, but sits neatly in a pot or tub looking pretty and restrained, then you might try Azalea, Hibiscus or Gardenia, with their large showy flowers, or the smaller Cyclamen, Streptocarpus (not a throat infection but an exotic primrose) and Vallota.

For a high-roofed, large conservatory, some tree specimens can be grown as standards in large tubs – lemon and orange trees, kumquats and palms such as the parlour palm (Chamaedorea elegans). These are true Victorian

conservatory plants, the very species that these buildings were designed and built for, the reason for their existence, and to have a conservatory that doesn't conserve at least one of them would be sacrilege.

Some will need some shade in summer from the worst of the sun and heat, but then, so will you. For sure, some of your plants will curl up and die, but others will take off as if they'd been returned to Eden, and finding out which will do which is

the pleasure of gardening. It's September and the last day of summer – the autumnal equinox. The sun is setting, and as it does so, it seems to draw the last warmth of summer down with it. You'd love to stay out in the garden, but there's a chill in the air. It matters not, for inside you have a room that is still filled with the heat of the sun and will be until it's time for bed – a room where you can still feel part of the garden and part of summer.

Blending aesthetically and functionally, a conservatory can become the most valuable addition to your home

167

Glossary

Btu British thermal unit (replaced by kilowatt).

Casement The hinged and opening part of a window.

Cavity closer Fitting or method of closing the cavity wall at peripheries of openings.

Cavity tray A tray-shaped damp-proof course installed to cavity walls over a junction with the roof.

Close-boarded roofs Where the rafters are clad tile side with timber boarding.

Cappings Finishing pieces to cover joints and ends.

Cold roof A roof that is insulated between the rafters or below them.

Coping Weathering stone or course to the top of a wall.

Corbelling Successive course-projecting brickwork.

Crack vent Window casement stay that keeps it slightly ajar.

Cresting Ornate ridge detail on a roof.

Derating Allowing for insulation overheating in electric cables.

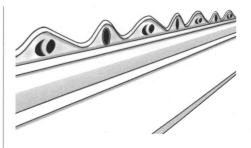

Cresting

Dessication Dried out subsoil causing shrinkage and subsidence.

Dentil course Projecting course of stone or brick.

DPM Damp-proof membrane beneath the base or slab finish.

Dummy bars Fake glazing bars in windows (sometimes between the panes of double-glazing).

Eaves The lower edge of the roof.

Fascia A horizontal decorative board fixed horizontally along the eaves to finish the roof edge.

Fenestration Architecture of windows.

Fielded panels Decorative relief work on wall panels.

Fenestration

Finials Pointed ornament on a gable end of a roof ridge.

Flashings Weathering between roof sheeting and wall.

Flemish bond Brick bond of alternate headers and stretchers in each course.

Fletton Cheap brick.

Glazing bars Slender sections used to support glass or plastic in windows or roofs.

Header The end face of a brick.

Horns Projection on the cill of a window or door frame to help build it into the wall.

Joist A horizontal structural member of a floor or ceiling.

Lead code The grade (thickness) of lead.

Lead rolls Wood core rolls dressed with lead.

Loop-in circuits Lighting circuit to reduce T-joints using ceiling roses.

Low-e glass Low-emissivity (reflective) coated double glazing.

Noggin A small piece of timber used between other main structural timbers to stiffen them.

Parapet A low wall on the edge of a roof, balcony or gutter.

Pitch The angle of a roof or rafters.

Quoin Brick or stone set in the corner of a wall.

Racking The result of wind pressure, causing a conservatory to lean.

Radial circuits A spur circuit leading off a ring circuit without looping back.

Rafters The sloping sections of a roof that support the glazing bars or tile battens.

Rapid ventilation By a window or door opening vent or an electric fan.

Ridge The apex of a roof.

SAP rating Standard Assessment Procedure figure for valuing the energy efficiency of a dwelling.

Snap header A half-brick (not a header).

Solvent-weld plumbing Glued permanent joints of plastic pipe.

Stucco Smooth external plastering.

Spalling Frost damage to bricks.

Soakaway A large hole or chamber for draining rainwater into the ground away from any building.

Soakers Undertile weatherings.

Solar gain Extent of potential additional heating caused by the sun.

Stretcher The long face of a brick.

Terrazzo Coloured floor mosaic.

Tie bar Steel bar between opposing walls or roof slopes installed to prevent them spreading apart.

Tusk tenon Small tenon joint (often used on stairwell trimmer to trimming joists).

Trickle vent Background vent that can be left open and is secure.

TRV Thermostatic radiator valve controlling radiator temperature.

U value A measure of thermal transmittance through an element.

Vertical DPC Damp-proof course incorporated within cavity closer.

Verge The edge of a roof along the gable end.

Voussoir A wedge-shaped arch brick.

Warm roof A roof that is insulated on the top rather than between the rafters or below them.

Wind post A vertical metal post incorporated within a wall structure to resist wind pressure.

Y junction A y-shaped drainage piece for joining one run to another.

Useful Contacts

BRE Scotland
01355 576200
www.bre.co.uk

British Interior Design Association
020 7349 0800
www.bida.org.uk

British Plastics Federation
020 7457 5000
www.bpf.co.uk

British Standards Institute
020 8996 9000
www.bsi.org.uk

British Woodworking Federation
020 7608 5050
www.bwf.co.uk

Building Centre (The)
020 7692 4000
www.buildingcentre.co.uk

Building Research Establishment
(BRE)
01923 6644000
www.bre.co.uk

Crime Concern
01793 863500
www.crimeconcern.org.uk

Federation of Master Builders
020 7242 7583
www.fmb.org

Georgian Group (The)
020 7529 8920
www.georgiangroup.org.uk

Heritage Building Contractors Group
01543 414234
www.buildingconservation.com

Institute of Plumbing
01708 472791
www.plumbers.org.uk

Lead Sheet Association
01892 822773
www.leadsheetassociation.org.uk

National Federation of Builders
020 7608 5000
www.theCC.org.uk

 **USEFUL CONTACTS**

National Inspection Council for Electrical Installation Contracting
020 7564 2323
www.niceic.org.uk

Plastic Window Federation
01582 456147
www.pwfed.co.uk

Royal Incorporation of Architects in Scotland (RIAS)
0131 229 7545
www.rias.org.uk

Royal Institution of British Architects (RIBA)
020 7580 5533
www.riba.org

Royal Institution of Chartered Surveyors (RICS)
020 7222 7000
www.rics.org.uk

Timber Research and Development Association (TRADA)
01494 569600
www.asktrada.co.uk

Victorian Society
020 8994 1019
www.victorian-society.org.uk

Glass and Glazing Federation (also FENSA and The Conservatory Association)
020 7681 2626/020 7207 5873

Index